RISING STARS
ASSESSMEN

Mathematics
Progress Tests

Year

5

Trevor Dixon
Series Advisors: Cornwall Learning

RISING★STARS

CORNWALL LEARNING

Rising Stars UK Ltd, 7 Hatchers Mews, Bermondsey Street, London SE1 3GS

www.risingstars-uk.com

First published 2014

Some material based on Rising Stars Assessment Mathematics Unit Tests Years
4–6 © Rising Stars 2008

Author: Trevor Dixon
Series advisors: Heather Davis and Maria Rundle, Cornwall Learning
Educational consultant: Sarah-Anne Fernandes
Editorial: Sparks Publishing Services, Gareth Fernandes
Typist: Rosalyn Dale
Design: Ray Rich and Clive Sutherland
Illustrations: Oxford Designers and Illustrators
Cover design: Burville-Riley Partnership

Rising Stars is grateful to the following people and schools who contributed to
the development of these materials.
Plumcroft Primary School, London; Rainford Brook Lodge Primary School,
Merseyside; St Nicholas CE Primary School, Chislehurst; St Margaret's CE
Primary School, Heywood, Rochdale; Tennyson Road Primary School, Luton

British Library Cataloguing in Publication Data.
A CIP record for this book is available from the British Library.
ISBN: 978 1 84680 952 1

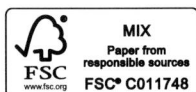

MIX
Paper from
responsible sources
FSC
www.fsc.org   FSC® C011748

Printed by Ashford Colour Press

Contents

Introduction

Why use Rising Stars Assessment Progress Tests?

The *Rising Stars Assessment Mathematics Progress Tests* have been developed to support teachers assess the progress their pupils are making against the 2014 National Curriculum Programme of Study for mathematics. The tests are designed to support effective classroom assessment across Years 1 to 6 and are easy to use and mark.

The tests are organised by the content domains in the Programme of Study and have been:
- written by primary mathematics assessment specialists
- reviewed by primary mathematics curriculum and assessment experts.

How do the tests track progress?

The results data from the tests can be used to track progress. They show whether pupils are making the expected progress for their year, more than expected progress or less than expected progress. This data can then be used alongside other evidence to enable effective planning of future teaching and learning, for reporting to parents and as evidence for Ofsted inspections. If teachers are using the CD-ROM version of the tests, the results data can be keyed into the Progress Tracker (see page 7 for more information) which automatically shows the progress of individual pupils against the Programme of Study and the results for all pupils by question and test. Data can also be exported into the school's management information system (MIS).

About the Mathematics Progress Tests

The tests are written to match the content requirements of the Programme of Study for the 2014 National Curriculum. The content areas are:

Content	Year 1	Year 2	Year 3	Year 4	Year 5	Year 6
Number: Number and place value	✓	✓	✓	✓	✓	✓
Number: Addition and subtraction	✓	✓	✓	✓	✓	✓
Number: Multiplication and division	✓	✓	✓	✓	✓	
Number: Fractions (*including* decimals (from Year 4) *and* percentages (from Year 5))	✓	✓	✓	✓	✓	✓
Ratio and proportion						✓
Algebra						✓
Measurement	✓	✓	✓	✓	✓	✓
Geometry (Properties of shapes *and* Position and direction)	✓	✓	✓	✓	✓	✓
Statistics		✓	✓	✓	✓	✓

For each content area there are five tests:
- Test 1(Low)
- Test 2(Medium)
- Test 3(Medium)
- Test 4(High)
- Test 5: Mental mathematics.

The marks for each test are as follows:

Test	Number of marks					
	Year 1	Year 2	Year 3	Year 4	Year 5	Year 6
Test 1(L)	10	10	12	12	15	15
Test 2(M)	10	10	12	12	15	15
Test 3(M)	10	10	12	12	15	15
Test 4(H)	10	10	12	12	15	15
Test 5: Mental mathematics	10	10	15	15	20	20

Test demand

The tests are pitched at different levels of demand and can be selected depending on the current attainment of pupils or according to how much of the topic has been taught.

Test 1 (Low) includes 50% questions assessing content from the year below the current year. This test is intended for use at the beginning of a topic. It may also be used with pupils who have not fully met the expectations of the previous year's Programme of Study.

Test 2 and Test 3 (Medium) both assess content from the current year only. These tests are intended for use during or at the end of the topic.

Test 4 (High) includes 50% questions assessing content from the year above the current year. It is designed for use with more able pupils or those demonstrating that they are making above expected progress in the topic. Test 4 could be used during or at the end of a topic.

Test 5: Mental mathematics tests are designed to be used by all pupils at the end of the topic and additionally provide the opportunity for pupils to practise the mental maths skills and test techniques they will need in end of key stage tests. These tests contain questions from the year below, the current year and the year above. The marks are split as follows:

	Number of marks		
	Year below	Current year	Year above
Years 1 and 2	2	6	2
Years 3 and 4	3	9	3
Years 5 and 6	5	10	5

Tracking progress

The marks pupils score in the tests can be used to track how they are progressing against the expected outcomes for their year group. The marks for each test have been split into three progress zones:
  • less than expected progress
  • expected progress
  • more than expected progress.

The zones for each year group are as follows:

	Test	Zone mark range		
		Less than expected progress	Expected progress	More than expected progress
Year 1	1–5	0–5	6–8	9–10
Year 2	1–5	0–5	6–8	9–10
Year 3	1–4	0–6	7–10	11–12
	5	0–7	8–12	13–15
Year 4	1–4	0–6	7–10	11–12
	5	0–7	8–12	13–15
Year 5	1–4	0–7	8–12	13–15
	5	0–10	11–16	17–20
Year 6	1–4	0–7	8–12	13–15
	5	0–10	11–16	17–20

The table gives the mark ranges for the progress zones for each test which you can use to see how well each pupil is doing in each test. If pupils are making the expected progress for their year they will be consistently scoring marks in the middle zone of marks in the tests. The higher the mark in the zone, the more secure you can be that they are making expected progress.

How to use the Mathematics Progress Tests

Preparation and timings

1 Make enough copies of the test(s) for each pupil to have their own copy. Note that the mental mathematics script containing the instructions for teachers is provided separately.

2 Hand out the papers and ensure pupils are seated appropriately so that they can't see each other's papers.

3 Pupils will need pens or pencils, rulers and erasers. Angle measurers should be available. Encourage pupils to cross out answers rather than rub them out.

4 There are no time limits for the tests but normal practice is to allow a minute per mark for written tests. Help with reading may be given using the same rules as when providing a reader with the DfE KS2 tests.

5 The mental mathematics tests should be strictly timed using a stopwatch or similar to provide practice for working under time constraints. *If you are using the CD-ROM version of the tests, an audio recording of the mental mathematics tests is provided. This includes a timed reading of the questions, making the tests particularly straightforward to administer.*

Supporting pupils during the tests

Before the test explain to the pupils that the test is an opportunity to show what they know, understand and can do. They should try to answer all the questions but should not worry if there are some they can't do.

Many pupils will be able to work independently in the tests, with minimal support from the teacher or a teaching assistant. However, pupils should be encouraged to 'have a go' at a question, or to move on to a fresh question if they appear to be stuck, to ensure that no pupil becomes distressed.

It is important that pupils receive appropriate support, but are not unfairly advantaged or disadvantaged. Throughout the tests, therefore, the teacher may read, explain or sign to a pupil any parts of the test that include instructions, for example by demonstrating how to circle an answer.

With younger age groups you may also consider using the version of the test on the CD-ROM and projecting it onto a whiteboard to support a whole class or group to take the tests. You may choose to refer to the words on the whiteboard and read them aloud so that pupils can follow them on the screen and on their own test paper and then write their answers on their papers individually.

Marking the tests

Use the detailed mark scheme and your professional judgement to award marks. Do not award half marks. Note that a number of questions in each test may require pupils to do more than one thing for one mark.

It is useful to use peer marking of test questions from time to time, particularly for the mental mathematics tests. Pupils should exchange test sheets and mark them as you read out the question and answer. You will need to check that pupils are marking accurately. This approach also provides an opportunity to recap on any questions that pupils found difficult to answer.

Feeding back to pupils

Once the test has been marked, use a five-minute feedback session with the pupils to help them review their answers. Wherever possible pupils should be encouraged to make their own corrections as in this way they will become more aware of their own strengths and weaknesses. A template Pupil progress sheet is provided on page 8 to help with this.

Using the Progress Tracker

The table on page 6 gives the mark ranges for the progress zones for each test which you can use to see how well each pupil is doing in each test. If pupils are making the expected progress for their year they will be consistently scoring marks in the middle zone of marks in the tests. The higher the mark in the zone, the more secure you can be that they are making expected progress.

The CD-ROM* version of *Mathematics Progress Tests* includes an interactive Progress Tracker, which allows you to enter the marks for each question for each test by pupil. This then automatically shows you which zone the pupil is in and also the zone distribution for the class so that you can track the progress of individual pupils and the whole class.

The Progress Tracker also enables you to review the marks for each question so that you can identify areas where some or all pupils may need further support and areas where some or all pupils are ready to be stretched further.

If required, data from the tests can be exported into the school's management information system (MIS) so that it can be used alongside other data in whole school monitoring including the monitoring of specific groups of pupils, such as Pupil Premium.

Full details about the Progress Tracker are provided on the CD-ROM.

* If you have the book version only of *Mathematics Progress Tests*, the Progress Tracker can be downloaded from bit.ly/progtracker

Pupil progress sheet

Name: _____ Class: _____ Date: _____

Topic name: _____ Test number: _____ My mark: _____

What I did well in the test:

_____

_____

_____

What I need to do to improve:

1. _____

2. _____

3. _____

✂ -

Pupil progress sheet

Name: _____ Class: _____ Date: _____

Topic name: _____ Test number: _____ My mark: _____

What I did well in the test:

_____

_____

_____

What I need to do to improve:

1. _____

2. _____

3. _____

Year 5
Number and place value   Test 1(L)

Name: _____ Class: _____ Date: _____

1. Which two numbers are missing from this sequence?

9, 18, 27, 36, _____, 54, 63, _____

2. What is 1000 more than 23 742?

_____

3. What are the next two numbers in this sequence?

28, 21, 14, 7, _____, _____

4. What is the value of the 6 in 7863?

_____

5. Put these numbers in order, smallest first.

5749   10 006   7081   6900

_____

6. What number is shown on this abacus?

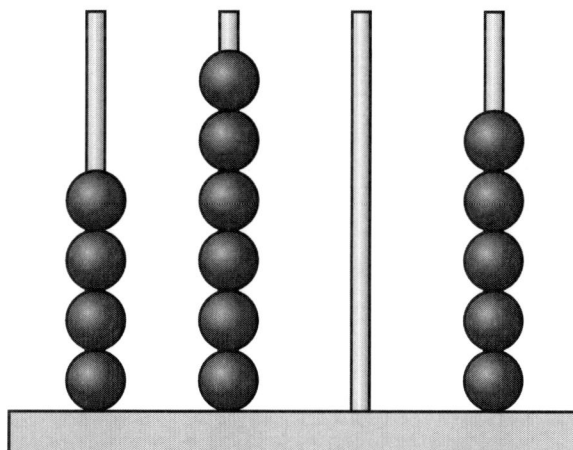

_____

7. Round 8075 to the nearest hundred.

_____

1 mark

8. Write twenty-seven thousand, six hundred and five in figures.

_____

1 mark

9. Which number comes next in this sequence?

456, 466, 476, 486, _____

1 mark

10. The temperature was –4°C.

The temperature rose by 6°C.

What is the temperature now?

°C

1 mark

11. The numbers in the squares are rounded to the nearest thousand.

Join the numbers in the squares to the number in the circle **if** they round to 15 000.

One has been done for you.

15 496   14 106   15 206

14 606   (15 000)   15 606

14 406   15 106   15 006

1 mark

Total for this page

12. Put these numbers in order, smallest first.

4   0   −4   5   −3

_____

1 mark

13. Here are four number cards.

Use all four cards to make the closest possible number to 5000.

(5)   (9)   (0)   (4)

_____

1 mark

14. What was the difference between the temperatures in London and Moscow on Wednesday?

Day	Temperature in London	Temperature in Moscow
Mon	4°C	−23°C
Tues	6°C	−19°C
Wed	5°C	−18°C

°C

1 mark

15. Change the Roman numeral CCLXXV to a number.

_____

1 mark

/15

Total for this test

Year 5
Number and place value   Test 2(M)

Name: _____ Class: _____ Date: _____

1. Write these numbers in order, largest first.

32 895   33 004   9879   29 860   30 928

_____

1 mark

2. Write 600 309 in words.

_____

1 mark

3. What is the next number in this sequence?

504 362   514 362   524 362   534 362   _____

1 mark

4. Jan adds one thousand to 736 296.
What is the answer?

_____

1 mark

5. I left the door of the freezer open. The temperature rose by 5°C.
What was the new temperature in the freezer?

	Temperature
fridge	4°C
freezer	−19°C

°C

1 mark

6. The arrow is pointing at −2.
Add 5. Draw a new arrow to show the answer.

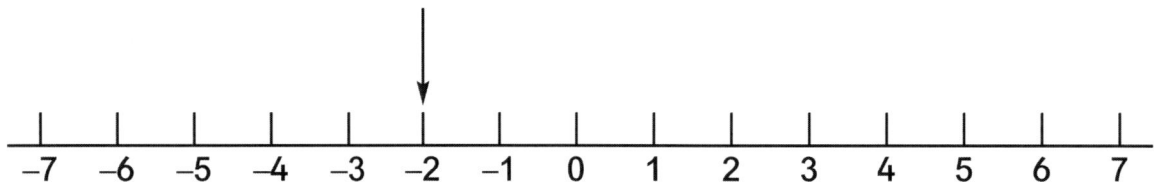

1 mark

Total for this page

12

7. The numbers on the left are to be rounded to the nearest thousand.
Join the number to its rounded number with a line.

169 489	167 000
167 231	168 000
167 601	169 000
170 654	170 000
169 654	171 000

1 mark

8. Sue rounds a number to the nearest 1000.
The rounded number is 53 000.
Which of these numbers did she round?
Circle the number.

53 695   52 498   5310   528 286   52 601

1 mark

9. Write the number that is 10 000 less than 1 000 000.

_____

1 mark

10. By how much is 357 787 larger than 356 787?

_____

1 mark

11. Round 843 708 to the nearest 10.

_____

1 mark

12. The temperature is shown on the thermometer.

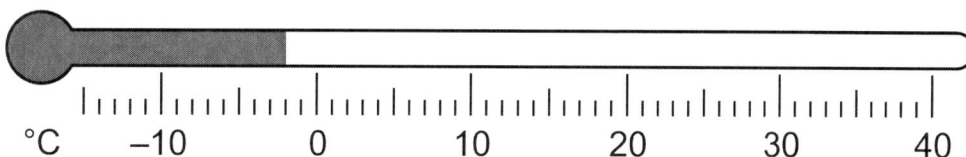

°C   −10   0   10   20   30   40

The temperature falls by 5°C.
What temperature will the thermometer show?

°C

1 mark

Total for this page

13. Circle the number that is closest to 420 000.

419 987   420 012   42 001   402 000   410 000

1 mark

14. What is the value of the number shown by the arrow?

940 578

↑   _____

1 mark

15. A house costs £345 000.

If the price rises by £10 000, what will the new price be?

£ _____

1 mark

/15

**Total for
this test**

Number and place value Test 3(M)

Name: _____ Class: _____ Date: _____

1. Circle the smallest number.

45 708   45 087   48 007   400 008   45 078

1 mark

2. Write six hundred and ten thousand four hundred in figures.

_____

1 mark

3. Write these numbers in order, smallest first.

4050   4005   4500   4070   4007

_____

1 mark

4. Write the number that is next in this sequence.

34 835   34 825   34 815   34 805   _____

1 mark

5. Mr. Dunn has £29 975 in his bank account.
He wins £100 and puts it into his bank account.
How much does he have now?

£ _____

1 mark

6. Which number is 100 000 smaller than 1 000 000?

_____

1 mark

7. What temperature does the thermometer show?

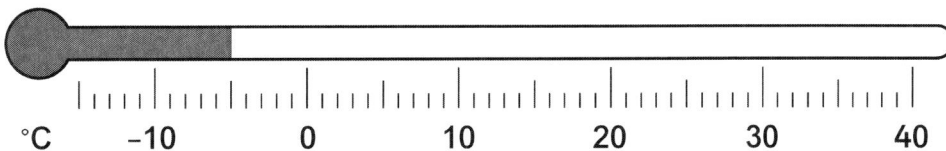

°C   −10   0   10   20   30   40

°C

1 mark

Total for this page

8. Temperature at:

noon   midnight

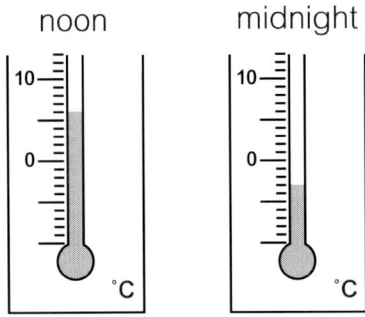

How many degrees did the temperature drop between noon and midnight?

| °C |

1 mark

9. Which two numbers come next in this sequence?

18   9   0   _____   _____

1 mark

10. Round 3423 to the nearest thousand and 289 to the nearest hundred, then multiply to find an approximate answer to 3423 × 289.

_____

1 mark

11. Complete this table by rounding 52 381.

	Rounded to the nearest 10	Rounded to the nearest 100	Rounded to the nearest 1 000
52 381			

2 marks

12. Which year is shown by MMVIII?

_____

1 mark

13. The crowd at a football match was 40 400.

On the news, this figure was given as 40 000.

Was the figure rounded to the nearest 10, 100 or 1000?

_____

1 mark

14. Write the number that has 1 unit, 3 hundreds, 8 thousands and 6 tens of thousands only.

_____

1 mark

/15

Total for this test

16

Year 5
Number and place value   Test 4(H)

Name: _____ Class: _____ Date: _____

---

1. 253 896

Which digit is worth tens of thousands?   _____

`1 mark`

---

2. 362 714

What is the value of the digit 7? _____

`1 mark`

---

3. The temperature in the freezer was –19°C.

The temperature in the fridge was 3°C.

What is the difference between the two temperatures?

[   ] °C

`1 mark`

---

4. In 2011, the population of Liverpool was 466 415.

What was this population to the nearest thousand?

_____

`1 mark`

---

5. Which year is shown as MCMXC in Roman numerals?

_____

`1 mark`

---

6. Arrange these place value cards to make a 6 digit number.

| 4 | 100 000 | 8000 | 700 |

_____

`1 mark`

---

7. Put these numbers in order, largest first.

–2   4   –10   7   –5

_____

`1 mark`

Total for
this page

8. Write nine million and nine thousand in numerals.

_____

1 mark

9. Round 4 752 736 to the nearest hundred thousand.

_____

1 mark

10. Calculate the difference between numbers shown by the two arrows.

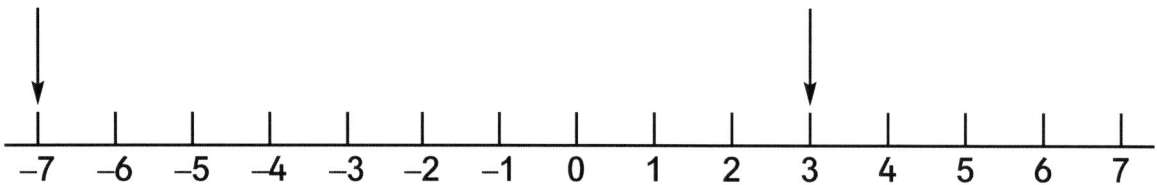

-7 -6 -5 -4 -3 -2 -1 0 1 2 3 4 5 6 7

_____

1 mark

11. Write these numbers in order, smallest first.

4 943 734   4 935 786   4 947 243   4 937 830

_____

1 mark

12. The lowest temperature ever recorded in UK was –26°C, the highest temperature ever recorded was 38°C. What is the difference between these temperatures?

°C

1 mark

13. Circle the largest number.

6 783 438   6 783 348   6 783 843   6 783 384

1 mark

14. Calculate:

–8 + 15

_____

1 mark

15. Round 6 820 198 to the nearest hundred.

_____

1 mark

/15

Total for this test

Year 5
Number and place value   Test 5: Mental mathematics

Instructions – to be read to pupils

Listen carefully to these instructions. I am going to ask you 20 questions. I will read each question twice. Listen carefully both times. You will then have time to work out your answer.

On your sheet there is an answer box for each question. Some questions are easy and some are harder. For some questions, important information is already written down for you on the sheet.

Work out the answer to each question in your head. Don't try to write down your calculations as this wastes time and you may miss the next question. If it helps you, you may jot things down outside the answer box.

If you can't work out an answer, put a cross in the answer box. If you make a mistake, cross out the wrong answer and then write the correct answer next to it.

You won't be able to ask questions once the test has begun. If you have any questions you may ask them now.

Now we are ready to start the test.

		Mark	Answer

For these questions, you will have 5 seconds to work out each answer and write it down.

		Mark	Answer
1.	Look at the numbers on your answer sheet. Write the next multiple of 7.	1	56
2.	Write the number that is 1000 less than 18 250.	1	17 250
3.	Look at your answer sheet. What is the value of the 6?	1	6000 or in words
4.	Look at your answer sheet. What is the value of the number shown using Roman numerals?	1	34
5.	Tom counts back 9 from 5. Which number does he count to?	1	−4

For these questions, you will have 10 seconds to work out each answer and write it down.

		Mark	Answer
6.	Write the number that is 10 000 more than 138 682.	1	148 682
7.	Write the number two hundred and fifty-seven thousand, three hundred and eighteen in figures.	1	257 318
8.	Round 467 000 to the nearest 100 000.	1	500 000 or in words
9.	Look at your answer sheet. Circle the number where the 7 is worth 70 000.	1	972 023
10.	The temperature in a greenhouse is 5 degrees Celsius, but outside the temperature is −3 degrees Celsius. What is the difference between the two temperatures?	1	8
11.	Look at your answer sheet. Circle the year that is the same as MLXVI in Roman numerals.	1	1066
12.	What number is 100 000 more than 5 900 000?	1	6 000 000
13.	Write any number rounded to the nearest 10 000 that comes between 351 600 and 388 700.	1	Accept any from: 360 000, 370 000, 380 000
14.	Look at your answer sheet. What is the next number in this sequence?	1	45 598
15.	What number is subtracted from 9 to give −12 as an answer?	1	21

For these questions, you will have 15 seconds to work out each answer and write it down.

		Mark	Answer
16.	Look at your answer sheet. Round 597 143 to the nearest 10 000.	1	600 000
17.	Write four million, three hundred and five thousand, six hundred and twenty in figures.	1	4 305 620
18.	What is 13 subtract 38?	1	−25
19.	The temperature at night was −6 degrees Celsius. The next day the temperature rose by 11 degrees Celsius. What was the daytime temperature?	1	5
20.	Look at your answer sheet. Circle the value of the number shown by the arrow.	1	50 000

Now put down your pen or pencil. The test is finished.

Year 5
Number and place value

Test 5: Mental mathematics

Name: _____ Class: _____ Date: _____

5-second questions

1.		28, 35, 42, 49

2.		18 250

3.		546 381

4.		XXXIV

5.		5

10-second questions

6.		138 682

7.		

8.		467 000

9.	897 231 703 459 972 023 45 709 12 670

10.		°C

11.	1516 1606 1066 1506 1046	MLXVI

12.		5 900 000

13.		351 600 388 700

14.		41 598 42 598 43 598 44 598

15.		9

15-second questions

16.		597 143

17.		

18.		13

19.		−6°C

20.	5 50 500 5000 50 000 500 000	3 459 126 ↑

Total for this test
/20

Year 5
Addition and subtraction Test 1(L)

Name: _____ Class: _____ Date: _____

1. Add 5000, 600, 90 and 7.

1 mark

2. Subtract 640 from 7000.

1 mark

3. Calculate 5672 + 3729.

1 mark

4. Calculate 8942 – 3898.

1 mark

Total for this page

5.   Write the missing number from this addition in the box.

$$
\begin{array}{ccc}
 & 5 & 7 & 3 \\
+ & 3 & \boxed{} & 9 \\
\hline
 & 9 & 6 & 2 \\
\end{array}
$$

□ 1 mark

6.   During the autumn term, a school kitchen cooked 9753 school dinners. In the spring term 8543 dinners were cooked and in the summer term were 7763 dinners cooked.

How many dinners were cooked in total?

□ 1 mark

7.   Daisy bought a car for £8499. Three years later she sold the car.

The car had lost £3749 in value. She used the remaining value and her savings of £5500 to buy her next car.

How much money did she have to spend?

£

□ 2 marks

□ Total for this page

8. Calculate 82 463 – 59 371.

1 mark

9. **a)** Round each number in the calculation 36 813 + 42 621 to the nearest thousand.
Add these rounded numbers to give an approximate answer.

1 mark

b) Calculate the actual total of 36 813 and 42 621.

1 mark

10. I am thinking of two numbers.
One of the numbers is 25 827.
The total of the two numbers is 84 381.
What is the other number?

_____

1 mark

Total for
this page

11. I am thinking of two numbers.

One of the numbers is 71 934.

The difference between this number and the other is 43 341.

What is the other number?

1 mark

12. Circle the number that can be added to 23 675 to give a total of 100 000.

67 425   76 325   76 425

77 325   87 435

1 mark

13. Which number comes halfway between 56 743 and 61 743?

_____

1 mark

/15

Total for this test

Year 5
Addition and subtraction Test 2(M)

Name: _____ Class: _____ Date: _____

1. Find the answer to 56 842 + 3100.

1 mark

2. Find the answer to 64 752 − 5690.

1 mark

3. Calculate 67 494 + 26 580.

1 mark

4. Calculate 70 742 − 29 837.

1 mark

Total for
this page

5. **a)** Round each number in the calculation 88854 − 56748 to the nearest ten thousand.

Subtract these rounded numbers to give an approximate answer.

1 mark

b) Calculate the actual difference between the two numbers.

1 mark

6. Calculate £3856.56 + £5673.78 + £347.45.

£

1 mark

7. At the beginning of the year, there was £7452.64 in the School Fund.

By the end of the year, £6845.46 had been spent.

How much was left in the School Fund?

£

1 mark

Total for this page

8. At a two-day summer fair, £12 645 was raised on the Saturday and £15 593 was taken on the Sunday.

At a two-day winter fair, £16 781 was raised on the Saturday and £10 286 was taken on the Sunday.

a) How much was raised at both fairs altogether?

£

1 mark

b) How much more was raised at the summer fair than at the winter fair?

£

1 mark

9. Here are some distances:

Journey	Distance (kilometres)
London to Rome	1431 km
London to Berlin	929 km
Berlin to Rome	1181 km

A plane flies from London to Rome and then on to Berlin.

How much further is this than flying direct to Berlin from London?

km

1 mark

Total for
this page

10. Write the missing numbers in this addition in the boxes.

$$
\begin{array}{cccccc}
 & \boxed{} & \boxed{7} & \boxed{} & \boxed{9} & \boxed{} \\
+ & \boxed{3} & \boxed{} & \boxed{7} & \boxed{} & \boxed{5} \\
\hline
 & \boxed{6} & \boxed{0} & \boxed{1} & \boxed{3} & \boxed{3} \\
\end{array}
$$

1 mark

11. 34 632 + 5832 + 9491

Round the numbers in this addition to the nearest thousand to find an estimated answer.

1 mark

12. A ship arrived at a port carrying 45 823 tonnes of cargo.

32 879 tonnes of cargo were unloaded.

The ship was then loaded with 42 734 tonnes before leaving port.

How much cargo was on the ship?

tonnes

2 marks

Total for this test

Year 5
Addition and subtraction   Test 3(M)

Name: _____ Class: _____ Date: _____

1. Find the answer to 326 253 + 14 972.

1 mark

2. Find the answer to 616 607 − 1309.

1 mark

3. Calculate 248 714 + 68 358.

1 mark

4. Calculate 813 742 − 153 614.

1 mark

Total for this page

5. Which number comes halfway between 52 400 and 100 000?

1 mark

6. **a)** Round each number in the calculation 712 288 – 138 867 to the nearest thousand.

Subtract these rounded numbers to give an approximate answer.

1 mark

b) Calculate the actual difference between 712 288 and 138 867.

1 mark

7. Add these lengths:

4675 km + 32 574 km + 328 567 km

km

1 mark

Total for
this page

8. The organisers of a concert raise £178 512 in ticket sales and £15 785 selling merchandise.

They have to pay the groups £45 750 and pay other expenses of £27 815.

How much money do they make for themselves?

£

2 marks

9. The populations of the three largest towns in a county were 435 167, 237 834 and 47 813.

What was the total population of these three cities?

1 mark

10. Find the number halfway between 125 000 and 850 000.

1 mark

11. Write the missing numbers in this subtraction in the boxes.

		9		1	
−	3		2		5
5	1	9	2	1	

1 mark

Total for
this page

12. A company has two factories that make mobile phones.

The company records the number of mobile phones made each year in a table.

	Hillsdon Factory	Green Vale Factory
2012	324 563	275 212
2013	285 713	412 067

a) How many more mobile phones were made in 2013 than in 2012 by the Green Vale Factory?

1 mark

b) How many more mobile phones were made by the Hillsdon Factory than the Green Vale Factory in 2012?

1 mark

/15

Total for this test

Year 5
Addition and subtraction   Test 4(H)

Name: _____ Class: _____ Date: _____

1. Find the answer to 513 753 + 73 000 + 8.

1 mark

2. Find the answer to 482 184 − 85 000.

1 mark

3. Calculate 718 482 + 443 628 + 53 672.

1 mark

4. Calculate 685 597 − 468 728.

1 mark

Total for
this page

5. Manisha adds three numbers together and gets the total 629 732.

Two of the numbers are 67 532 and 483 817.

What is the third number?

1 mark

6. Use rounding to the nearest ten thousand to find an estimated answer to:

56 831 + 48 832 + 31 742 + 83 184

1 mark

7. A factory has a stock of 51 763 boxes.

35 609 boxes are used.

How many boxes are left?

1 mark

Total for
this page

8. A football stadium has 48 523 seats.

24 632 of the seats are used by season ticket holders, 1655 seats are in boxes and 1476 are used by guests of the club.

How many seats are available for sale?

2 marks

9. A car dealer checks his stock of cars. He has 6 cars for sale.

The prices of the cars are:

£5000, £6700, £8400, £11 450, £13 450 and £14 400.

He sells two cars and the total value of his stock is now £40 000.

What was the value of each of the two cars he sold?

£ _____ and £ _____

2 marks

Total for this page

10. Dev buys a round-the-world airline ticket and books these flights.

Journey	Distance in kilometres
London, UK to Hong Kong	9646
Hong Kong to Sydney, Australia	7349
Sydney, Australia to Rio de Janeiro, Brazil	13538
Rio de Janeiro, Brazil to Los Angeles, USA	10128
Los Angeles, USA to London, UK	8778

How far did Dev fly in total?

km

1 mark

11. Katy adds 587832, 672721 and 281465.

To check, she rounds the numbers to the nearest hundred thousand.

She says, 'My answer should be about 1300000.'

What mistake could Katy have made in her rounding?

1 mark

Total for this page

12. A builder turns an old house into four flats.

He sells them for £125 500, £135 750, £149 900 and £155 000.

But he had to pay £375 000 to buy the house, he paid his workers £37 675 and he had to pay £85 672 for materials.

How much money did he make?

£

2 marks

/15

Total for this test

Year 5
Addition and subtraction   Test 5: Mental mathematics

Instructions – to be read to pupils

Listen carefully to these instructions. I am going to ask you 20 questions. I will read each question twice. Listen carefully both times. You will then have time to work out your answer.

On your sheet there is an answer box for each question. Some questions are easy and some are harder. For some questions, important information is already written down for you on the sheet.

Work out the answer to each question in your head. Don't try to write down your calculations as this wastes time and you may miss the next question. If it helps you, you may jot things down outside the answer box.

If you can't work out an answer, put a cross in the answer box. If you make a mistake, cross out the wrong answer and then write the correct answer next to it.

You won't be able to ask questions once the test has begun. If you have any questions you may ask them now.

Now we are ready to start the test.

		Mark	Answer

For these questions, you will have 5 seconds to work out each answer and write it down.

		Mark	Answer
1.	Add 210 and 480.	1	690
2.	Subtract 310 from 750.	1	440
3.	What is added to 6100 to get a total of 8300?	1	2200
4.	What is subtracted from 12 000 to get 8400?	1	3600
5.	Find the total of 5000, 5700 and 5400.	1	16 100

For these questions, you will have 10 seconds to work out each answer and write it down.

		Mark	Answer
6.	What is 65 000 plus 9700?	1	74 700
7.	What is 32 500 minus 4600?	1	27 900
8.	What is added to 630 000 to get 1 000 000?	1	370 000
9.	What would be subtracted from 750 000 to get 590 000?	1	160 000
10.	Add 1 100 000 to 230 000.	1	1 330 000
11.	Which number is 50 000 fewer than 900 000?	1	850 000
12.	Find the difference between 100 000 and 11 000.	1	89 000
13.	Subtract 3984 from 4013.	1	29
14.	What is the difference between 6993 and 8007?	1	1014
15.	What is 3012 minus 2997?	1	15

For these questions, you will have 15 seconds to work out each answer and write it down.

		Mark	Answer
16.	What is the total of 3 400 000 and 800 000?	1	4 200 000
17.	What is added to 750 000 to get 5 000 000?	1	4 250 000
18.	Find the difference between 6 000 000 and 60 000.	1	5 940 000
19.	Find the sum of 2 200 000 and 22 000.	1	2 222 000
20.	What is 5 000 000 minus 550 000?	1	4 450 000

Now put down your pen or pencil. The test is finished.

Year 5
Addition and subtraction

Test 5: Mental mathematics

Name: _____ Class: _____ Date: _____

5-second questions

1.		480

2.		750

3.		6100

4.		12 000

5.		

10-second questions

6.		65 000

7.		32 500

8.		630 000

9.		750 000

10.	

11.	

12.		

13.		3984 4013

14.		6993 8007

15.		2997 3012

15-second questions

16.	

17.	

18.	

19.	

20.	

Total for this test
/20

Year 5
Multiplication and division Test 1(L)

Name: _____ Class: _____ Date: _____

1. **a)** Use the number cards to make a correct multiplication fact.

| 1 | 2 | 3 | 4 |

⬜ × ⬜ = ⬜⬜

b) Use the number cards to make a correct multiplication fact.

| 5 | 6 | 7 | 8 |

⬜ × ⬜ = ⬜⬜

2. Calculate 384×6.

3. Calculate $576 \div 6$.

4. Find the missing number.

$$\boxed{} \div 4 = 234$$

5. Find the missing number.

$$\boxed{} \times 7 = 868$$

6. Tins of soup are packed in boxes of 48.

How many tins of soup are in 8 boxes?

7. There are 6 felt tips in a pack.

How many packs can be filled from 672 felt tips?

8. Write in the missing factors of 20.

1					20

9. Write all the numbers that are factors of both 24 and 30.

_____

Total for
this page

10. Circle the prime numbers.

41   42   43   44   45   46   47   48   49

1 mark

11. Calculate $4704 \div 8$.

1 mark

12. Calculate $5^2 + 5^3$.

1 mark

13. The exchange rate between pounds and euros is:

£1 = €1.25

How many euros would you get if you exchanged £75?

.   €

1 mark

14. Write the missing number in the box:

$2250 \times 10 = 22\,500$

So

$2250 \times 70 = 22\,500 \times$

1 mark

/15

Total for this test

Year 5
Multiplication and division Test 2(M)

Name: _____ Class: _____ Date: _____

1. Write all the numbers that are factors of both 24 and 32.

_____

1 mark

2. Write two numbers that are multiples of both 8 and 6.

[ ] and [ ]

1 mark

3. Write one digit in each box to make this number sentence correct.

[ ][ ] × [ ] = 150

1 mark

4. Calculate 4689 × 8.

1 mark

5. Calculate 7776 ÷ 6.

1 mark

6. Circle the prime numbers.

51   52   53   54   55   56   57   58   59

1 mark

Total for this page

7. Write the missing number in the box.

$$45.6 \times 100 = \boxed{} \div 100$$

1 mark

8. A factory puts 8 packets of crisps in a large bag.

There are 2500 packets of crisps.

How many large bags can be filled?

1 mark

9. A school can organise the pupils into three teams or four teams for its sports day.

If they use four teams, there are 192 pupils in a team.

If they use three teams, how many pupils would be in a team?

2 marks

10. Circle all the numbers that are divisible by 3.

13   20   36

163   225

1 mark

Total for this page

11. Write the missing numbers in this multiplication in the boxes.

$$\begin{array}{ccccc} \boxed{} & \boxed{7} & \boxed{} & & \boxed{} \\ & & & & \boxed{7} \\ \times & 5 & 2 & 5 & \\ \hline \boxed{3} & \boxed{3} & \boxed{} & \boxed{6} & \boxed{6} \end{array}$$

1 mark

12. Find **two** pairs of prime numbers that add together to make 20.

_____ and _____

_____ and _____

1 mark

13. Sally knows that:

$34\,500 \times 100 = 3\,450\,000$

Explain how she could use this fact to calculate:

$34\,500 \times 250$

_____

_____

_____

1 mark

14. Calculate $1^2 + 2^2 + 3^2 + 4^2$.

1 mark

/15

Total for this test

Year 5
Multiplication and division   Test 3(M)

Name: _____ Class: _____ Date: _____

1. Write all the numbers from 2 to 9 in the correct places on the Carroll diagram. One is done for you.

2̸   3   4   5   6   7   8   9

	Multiple of 3	Not a multiple of 3
Factor of 24		2
Not a factor of 24		

2 marks

2. Circle all the numbers that are wholly divisible by 7 and 8.

280   320   420   560   720   1120

1 mark

3. Calculate 6274 × 53.

1 mark

4. Calculate 5062 ÷ 8.

1 mark

Total for this page

5. Write the prime factors of 30.

_____

1 mark

6. Change the units of these metric measures.

a) 5.5 kg = _____ g

b) 6.7 m = _____ cm

1 mark

7. A recipe for making lemonade for 4 people uses:
- 1 000 ml of mineral water
- 100 g of sugar
- 80 ml of lemon juice

Rewrite the recipe for 10 people.

_____ ml of mineral water

_____ g of sugar

_____ ml of lemon juice

1 mark

8. A school has £5740 to spend on 7 classes to buy books and equipment.

An eighth class, the nursery class has £1175 to spend on books and equipment.

How much more does the nursery class get than any of the other classes in the school?

£

1 mark

Total for this page

9. Use each number **once** to make **all** these sentences correct.

27   64   81

	is a square number
	is a cube number
	is both a square and a cube number

1 mark

10. $675 \times 8 = 5400$

Use this fact to calculate:

675×12

Show your working.

1 mark

11. Pencils come in packs of 8.

A school has 587 children.

How many packs will a school need to buy so each child can have a pencil?

1 mark

Total for this page

12. A factory makes 3400 sweets an hour.

The sweets are put into packs of 9.

How many full packs will there be?

1 mark

13. A factory fills 7948 cans of drink in an hour.

How many cans will be filled in 7 hours?

1 mark

14. A school spends £5800 on books for 8 classes.

How much is spent on books for each class?

£

1 mark

/15

**Total for
this test**

Multiplication and division   Test 4(H)

Name: _____ Class: _____ Date: _____

1. Write one number that fits all three of these statements:
- It is a multiple of 6.
- It is a multiple of 8.
- It ends in a 4.

1 mark

2. Calculate 7352 × 73.

1 mark

3. Calculate 8379 ÷ 6.

1 mark

4. A sports club holds a charity weekend.

They raised £3756 on Saturday and £5187 on Sunday.

The club decides to share the money between three different charities.

How much money will each charity get?

£

1 mark

Total for this page

5. Write all the prime numbers between 10 and 20.

_____

1 mark

6. Write all the factors of 42.

_____

2 marks

7. Use long multiplication to calculate:

6385×48

Show your working.

1 mark

8. Calculate:

$4688 \div 32$

Show your working.

1 mark

9. Circle the common multiples of 7 and 8.

78   210   560   630   700   728

1 mark

10. Calculate:

$56 \times (5463 + 302)$

1 mark

Total for this page

11. Mr Jones runs two shops.

He compares the takings of the two shops for January and February.

	Shop 1	Shop 2
January	£3721	£4423
February	£4984	£4174

a) Which shop took the most money and by how much?

Shop   by £

1 mark

b) Use these figures to calculate how much Mr Jones may expect to take from both shops for the whole year.

£

1 mark

Total for this page

12. 6784 x 63

a) Round these numbers to the nearest thousand and the nearest 10 to calculate an estimated answer.

1 mark

b) Use long multiplication to calculate the exact answer.

1 mark

/15

Total for this test

Year 5
Multiplication and division Test 5: Mental mathematics

Instructions – to be read to pupils

Listen carefully to these instructions. I am going to ask you 20 questions. I will read each question twice. Listen carefully both times. You will then have time to work out your answer.

On your sheet there is an answer box for each question. Some questions are easy and some are harder. For some questions, important information is already written down for you on the sheet.

Work out the answer to each question in your head. Don't try to write down your calculations as this wastes time and you may miss the next question. If it helps you, you may jot things down outside the answer box.

If you can't work out an answer, put a cross in the answer box. If you make a mistake, cross out the wrong answer and then write the correct answer next to it.

You won't be able to ask questions once the test has begun. If you have any questions you may ask them now.

Now we are ready to start the test.

		Mark	Answer

For these questions, you will have 5 seconds to work out each answer and write it down.

		Mark	Answer
1.	What is 56 divided by 8?	1	7
2.	What is 400 multiplied by 6?	1	2400
3.	Look at your answer sheet. Circle the pair of numbers that are both factors of 54.	1	6 and 9 identified only
4.	Multiply 2 by 2 by 4.	1	16
5.	What is 84 divided by 7?	1	12

For these questions, you will have 10 seconds to work out each answer and write it down.

		Mark	Answer
6.	Look at your answer sheet. Circle the number that is not a factor of 36.	1	5
7.	What is 720 divided by 8?	1	90
8.	What is 90 divided by 6?	1	15
9.	What is half of 188?	1	94
10.	Tickets cost 5 pounds each. Alan has 37 pounds. How many tickets can he buy?	1	7
11.	Pencils cost 49 pence each. Fay has 10 pounds. How many pencils can Fay buy?	1	20
12.	What is 36 multiplied by 10?	1	360
13.	Divide 32 by 100.	1	0.32
14.	What is six squared minus two squared?	1	32
15.	What is ninety squared?	1	8100

For these questions, you will have 15 seconds to work out each answer and write it down.

		Mark	Answer
16.	Multiply 70 by 40.	1	2800
17.	Look at your answer sheet. Circle the prime number.	1	59
18.	Divide 12 000 by 500.	1	24
19.	Look at your answer sheet. Circle the number that is **not** a factor of 72.	1	14
20.	Multiply 20 by 60, then divide the answer by 40.	1	30

Now put down your pen or pencil. The test is finished.

Year 5
Multiplication and division

Test 5: Mental mathematics

Name: _____ Class: _____ Date: _____

5-second questions

1.	

2.		46

3.	6 and 8 6 and 9 7 and 9 2 and 38

4.	

5.	

10-second questions

6.	2 3 4 5 6

7.		720

8.	

9.		188

10.	

11.		49p

12.	

13.	

14.	

15.	

15-second questions

16.	

17.	51 57 59 69 81

18.	

19.	4 6 8 14 24

20.	

Total for this test

/20

Year 5
Fractions, decimals and percentages   Test 1(L)

Name: _____ Class: _____ Date: _____

1. Find $\frac{3}{4}$ of 32.

_____

2. Calculate $\frac{9}{10} - \frac{7}{10}$.

_____

3. 45 is divided by 100.

What is the value of the 4 in the answer?

Circle the correct answer.

4 units   4 tenths   4 hundreths   4 thousandths

4. Each decimal number is rounded to the nearest whole number.

Draw a line from the decimal number to the correct rounded number.
The first one is done for you.

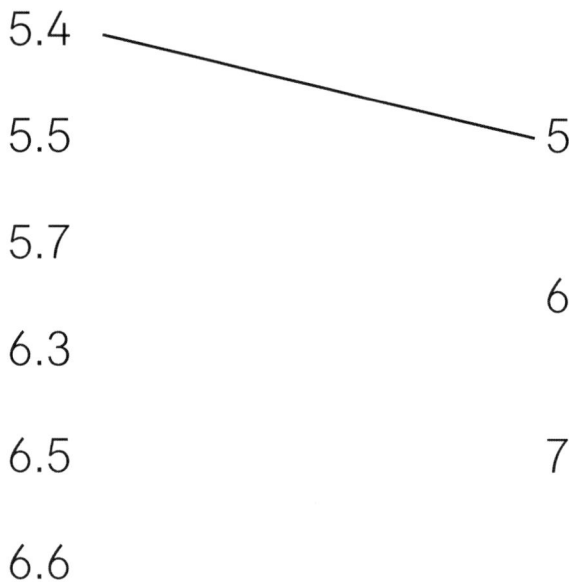

5.4 ———————

5.5   5

5.7

                       6

6.3

6.5   7

6.6

5. Write these numbers in order, largest first.

12.48   12.43   11.96   12.64   13.12

_____

6.   Dave orders 6 pizzas for himself and three friends.

They share the pizzas equally.

How much do they each get?

_____

1 mark

7.   Draw a line to match these decimals to their fraction equivalents.

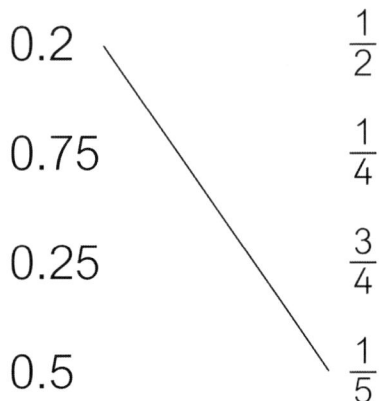

0.2 $\frac{1}{2}$

0.75 $\frac{1}{4}$

0.25 $\frac{3}{4}$

0.5 $\frac{1}{5}$

1 mark

8.   Put these fractions in order, smallest first.

$\frac{2}{3}$ $\frac{5}{6}$ $\frac{7}{12}$ $\frac{19}{24}$

_____

1 mark

9.   Use the diagram to help find the missing number.

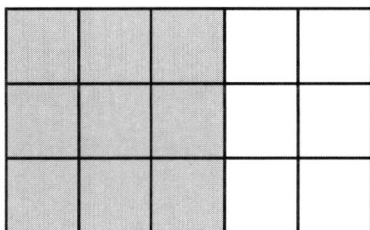

$$\frac{9}{15} = \frac{\boxed{}}{5}$$

1 mark

Total for this page

10. Match each box to the fraction that has the same value.

One has been done for you.

$\frac{2}{4}$

$\frac{5}{4}$

$\frac{3}{4}$

$\frac{1}{4}$

$1\frac{1}{4}$

$\frac{1}{2}$

$\frac{5}{8}$

$\frac{3}{12}$

$\frac{6}{8}$

2 marks

11. Calculate:

$\frac{3}{4} + \frac{3}{8}$

_____

1 mark

12. Write 0.23 as a fraction.

_____

1 mark

13. Calculate:

$336 + 1.7 + 26.51 =$ ⬚

1 mark

14. What percentage of the bar is shaded?

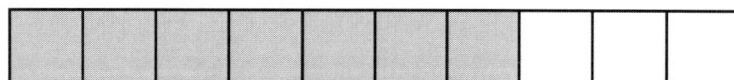

_____ %

1 mark

/15

Total for this test

58

Year 5
Fractions, decimals and percentages   Test 2(M)

Name: _____ Class: _____ Date: _____

1. Write these fractions in order, largest first.

$\frac{3}{4}$ $\frac{7}{8}$ $\frac{1}{2}$ $\frac{11}{16}$

_____

1 mark

2. The rectangle is divided into 100 smaller rectangles.

Write missing numbers in the boxes that show the value of the shaded area.

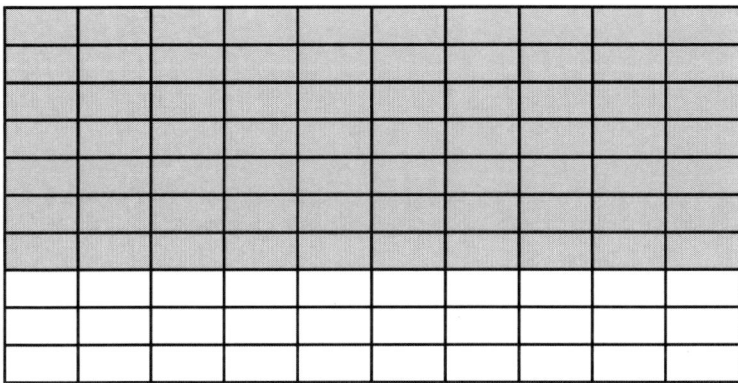

$$\frac{\boxed{}}{100} = \frac{\boxed{}}{10}$$

1 mark

3. Complete the table.

One is done for you.

Improper fraction	Mixed number
$\frac{5}{4}$	$1\frac{1}{4}$
	$3\frac{5}{6}$
$\frac{42}{5}$	

2 marks

4. Calculate:

$\frac{7}{12} - \frac{1}{4}$

_____

1 mark

Total for this page

5. Calculate:

$$\frac{2}{5} \times 4$$

Write your answer as a mixed number.

_____

1 mark

6. Circle **all** the fractions that are the same as 0.5.

$$\frac{0}{5} \qquad \frac{1}{5} \qquad \frac{1}{2} \qquad \frac{5}{10} \qquad \frac{50}{100}$$

1 mark

7. Write the missing numbers on the number line.

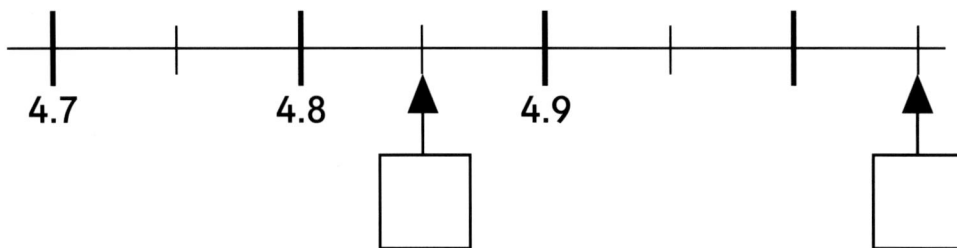

1 mark

8. Round these decimals to one decimal place.

7.84 ⟶ ☐

3.19 ⟶ ☐

1 mark

9. Circle the bigger number.

13.3   13.13

Explain how you know.

_____

_____

1 mark

Total for this page

10. Calculate:

$68.9 + 3.47 =$ ☐

1 mark

11. What is 50p as a percentage of £10?

☐ %

1 mark

12. Work out 25% of £200.

£ ☐

1 mark

13. Calculate $87.6 \div 6$

☐

1 mark

14. Put these decimals in order of size, smallest first.

0.211   0.122   0.212   0.102   0.201

_____

1 mark

/15

Total for this test

Year 5
Fractions, decimals and percentages   Test 3(M)

Name: _____ Class: _____ Date: _____

1. Circle the largest fraction.

$\dfrac{2}{5}$ $\dfrac{3}{10}$ $\dfrac{7}{15}$ $\dfrac{13}{20}$

1 mark

2.

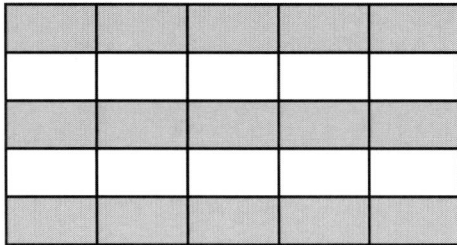

Use the diagram to complete this number sentence.

$\dfrac{10}{25} = \dfrac{\boxed{}}{5}$

1 mark

3. The improper fraction $\frac{7}{5}$ written as a mixed number is $1\frac{2}{5}$.

Write the improper fraction below as a mixed number.

$\dfrac{19}{8} = $ _____

1 mark

4. Calculate:

$\dfrac{3}{4} + \dfrac{1}{2} + \dfrac{1}{8}$

Write your answer as a mixed number.

_____

1 mark

5. Calculate:

$2\frac{1}{2} \times 3 = \boxed{}$

1 mark

Total for this page

6. Circle the fraction that is the same as 0.05.

$\frac{5}{10}$ $\frac{1}{5}$ $\frac{5}{100}$ $\frac{5}{0}$ $\frac{100}{5}$

1 mark

7. Change 0.639 into three fractions.

$0.639 = \dfrac{\boxed{}}{1000} + \dfrac{\boxed{}}{100} + \dfrac{\boxed{}}{10}$

1 mark

8. Circle the numbers that round to 15.

15.6   15.49   14.09   14.7   14.15

1 mark

9. Write these numbers in order of size, starting with the smallest.

3.137   3.37   0.731   0.71   3.7

smallest   **largest**

1 mark

10. A bucket holds 9.7 litres of water.
How much do 8 buckets hold?

litres

1 mark

11. Becky shared a chocolate bar with her two friends.
She gave 40% to Ella and 25% to Ben.
What percentage did she keep?

%

1 mark

Total for
this page

12. Complete the table.

Fraction	Decimal	Percentage
$\frac{1}{2}$	0.5	50%
		25%
$\frac{2}{5}$		

2 marks

13. Write $\frac{3}{4}$ as a decimal and as a percentage.

_____   _____ %

1 mark

14. Calculate:

$\frac{11}{12} - \frac{1}{6}$

_____

1 mark

/15

Total for this test

Year 5
Fractions, decimals and percentages   Test 4(H)

Name: _____ Class: _____ Date: _____

1. Write these fractions in order, smallest first.

$\frac{5}{12}$ $\frac{9}{24}$ $\frac{1}{3}$ $\frac{1}{6}$

_____

1 mark

2. Each of the missing denominators is the same number.

What is the missing denominator?

$\dfrac{3}{\Box} + \dfrac{4}{\Box} = \dfrac{7}{\Box} = 1\dfrac{2}{\Box}$

1 mark

3. Write 0.8 as a fraction.

_____

1 mark

4. These decimals are rounded to 1 decimal place.

Circle the decimals that can be rounded to 14.3.

14.35   14.24   14.03   14.28   14.34

1 mark

5. Below is part of a number line.

Write the decimal that the arrow points to.

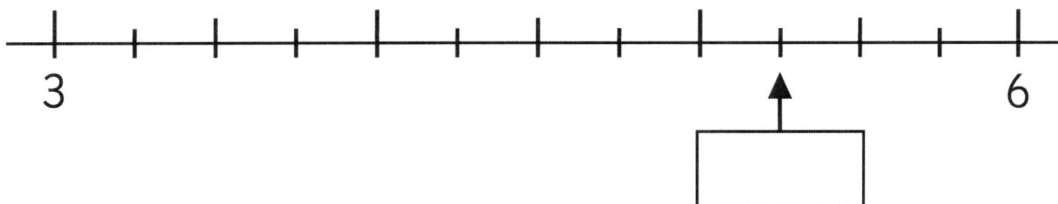

1 mark

Total for
this page

6. $178.2 \div 6 =$

1 mark

7. Calculate 75% of £800.

£

1 mark

8. Circle all the fractions that can be simplified to $\frac{2}{3}$.

$$\frac{10}{15} \qquad \frac{9}{12} \qquad \frac{14}{20} \qquad \frac{16}{24} \qquad \frac{12}{18}$$

1 mark

9. Calculate $4\frac{1}{2} + 3\frac{2}{5}$.

1 mark

10. Calculate $\frac{2}{3} \times \frac{4}{5}$.

1 mark

11. Calculate $\frac{1}{4} \div 3$.

1 mark

Total for this page

12. Change $\frac{1}{8}$ into a decimal.

1 mark

13. Complete this table.
One has been done for you.

	÷10	÷100
45.2	4.52	0.452
307.4		
72		

1 mark

14. Complete this table.
One has been done for you.

	×10	×100
5.6	56	560
0.603		
2.007		

1 mark

15. Write these mixed numbers in order, smallest first.

$2\frac{1}{2}$ $1\frac{3}{4}$ $2\frac{1}{4}$ $2\frac{3}{4}$ $2\frac{5}{8}$

_____

1 mark

/15

Total for this test

Year 5
Fractions, decimals and percentages Test 5: Mental mathematics

Instructions – to be read to pupils

Listen carefully to these instructions. I am going to ask you 20 questions. I will read each question twice. Listen carefully both times. You will then have time to work out your answer.

On your sheet there is an answer box for each question. Some questions are easy and some are harder. For some questions, important information is already written down for you on the sheet.

Work out the answer to each question in your head. Don't try to write down your calculations as this wastes time and you may miss the next question. If it helps you, you may jot things down outside the answer box.

If you can't work out an answer, put a cross in the answer box. If you make a mistake, cross out the wrong answer and then write the correct answer next to it.

You won't be able to ask questions once the test has begun. If you have any questions you may ask them now.

Now we are ready to start the test.

		Mark	Answer

For these questions, you will have 5 seconds to work out each answer and write it down.

		Mark	Answer
1.	Add three-twelfths and eight-twelfths.	1	$\frac{11}{12}$
2.	Write twenty-three hundredths as a decimal.	1	0.23
3.	Round 37.7 to the nearest whole number.	1	38
4.	What is 10 per cent of 2 pounds, 50 pence?	1	25p
5.	Write 20 per cent as a fraction.	1	$\frac{20}{100}$ or $\frac{2}{10}$ or $\frac{1}{5}$

For these questions, you will have 10 seconds to work out each answer and write it down.

		Mark	Answer
6.	Divide 4 by 100. Write the answer as a decimal.	1	0.04
7.	Look at your answer sheet. Circle the largest number.	1	4.7
8.	Carla spends 6 pounds, 15 pence. How much change would she get from 20 pounds?	1	£13.85
9.	Write 7.5 as a mixed number.	1	$7\frac{1}{2}$ or $7\frac{5}{10}$
10.	What is two and three-eighths as an improper fraction?	1	$\frac{19}{8}$
11.	Look at your answer sheet. Circle the largest number.	1	3.7
12.	What is two fifths as a percentage?	1	40%
13.	Look at your answer sheet. Circle the smallest fraction.	1	$\frac{3}{8}$
14.	Take one-half from eleven-twelfths.	1	$\frac{5}{12}$
15.	Divide one-half by five.	1	$\frac{1}{10}$

For these questions, you will have 15 seconds to work out each answer and write it down.

		Mark	Answer
16.	What is 8.1 minus 1.8?	1	6.3
17.	Look at your answer sheet. Circle the fraction that is twenty twenty-fourths simplified.	1	$\frac{5}{6}$
18.	Multiply 60.708 by 1000.	1	60 708
19.	Add five and one-quarter and three and one-half.	1	$8\frac{3}{4}$
20.	What is four-fifths written as a decimal?	1	0.8

Now put down your pen or pencil. The test is finished.

Year 5
Fractions, decimals and percentages
Test 5: Mental mathematics

Name:	Class:	Date:

5-second questions

1.		$\frac{8}{12}$

2.		$\frac{23}{100}$

3.		37.7

4.		£2.50

5.		20%

10-second questions

6.	

7.	4.48 4.09 4.60 4.5 4.7

8.		£6.15

9.	

10.		$2\frac{3}{8}$

11.	3.7 1.37 3.337 3.37 1.373

12.	

13.	$\frac{7}{8}$	$\frac{3}{4}$	$\frac{5}{8}$	$\frac{3}{8}$	$\frac{1}{2}$

14.		$\frac{11}{12}$

15.		$\frac{1}{2}$

15-second questions

16.		8.1

17.	$\frac{4}{5}$	$\frac{5}{6}$	$\frac{5}{7}$	$\frac{7}{8}$	$\frac{10}{14}$

18.		60.708

19.	

20.		$\frac{4}{5}$

Total for this test
/20

Name: _____ Class: _____ Date: _____

1. Sumita says, 'I run 5000 metres every day.'

How many kilometres (km) does she run in a week?

_____ km

2. Work out the perimeter of this rectangle.

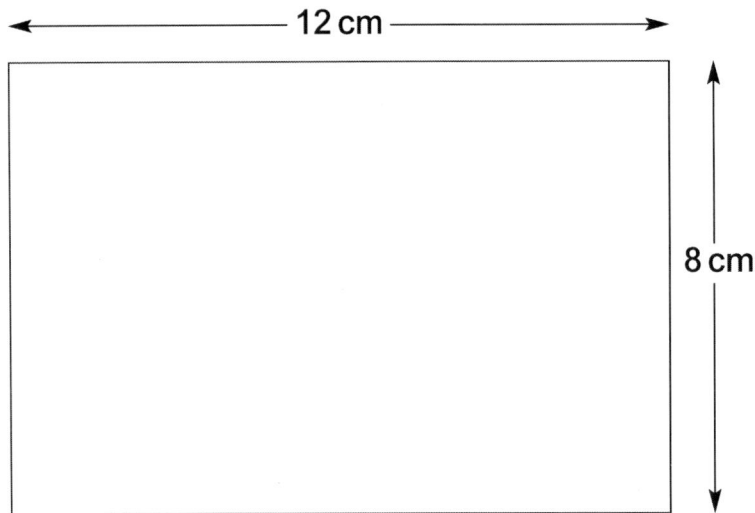

12 cm

8 cm

cm

3. This shape is drawn on centimetre squared paper.

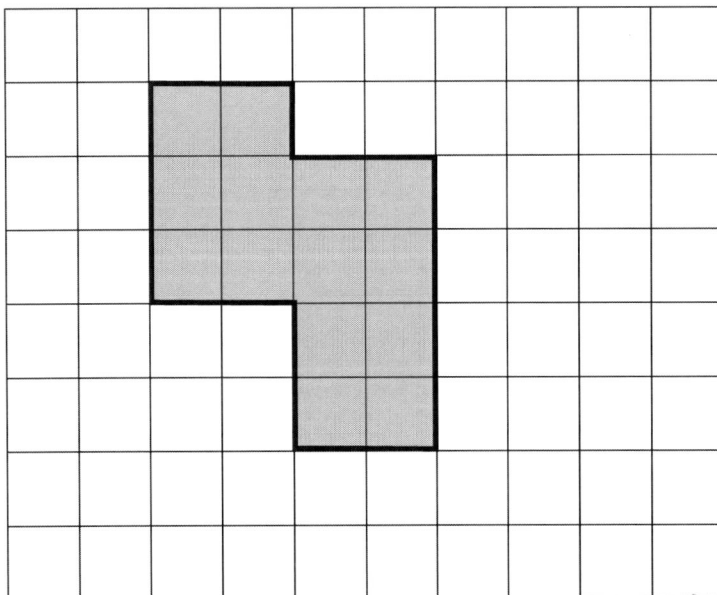

Work out the area of the shape.

cm²

4. A can of drink contains 330 ml.
How many millilitres of drink are there in a pack of six cans?

_____ ml

1 mark

5. A film started at 18:15 and finished at 20:35.
Change both these times into 12-hour digital time.

A film started at _____ and finished at _____.

1 mark

6. Denis says, 'I'm going away for three weeks.'
How many days will he be away?

_____ days

1 mark

7. Circle the largest capacity:

$3.2\,l$ $3\frac{1}{4}\,l$ $3.04\,l$ $3\,100\,ml$ $3\,l$

1 mark

8. Ravi said, '6 kg is 10 times heavier than 0.6 kg.'
Is he correct? Circle one.

YES   NO

Explain your answer.

_____

_____

_____

1 mark

9.

| 12 inches = 1 foot = 30 cm. |

Mr Biswas is 5 feet 6 inches tall.
What is Mr Biswas's height in metres?

m

2 marks

Total for this page

10. The pentagon shape is made with a square and an equilateral triangle, so all sides are the same length.

The perimeter of the equilateral triangle is 36 cm.

What is the perimeter of the pentagon?

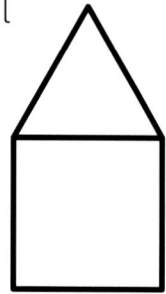

| cm |

1 mark

11. What is the area of this shape?

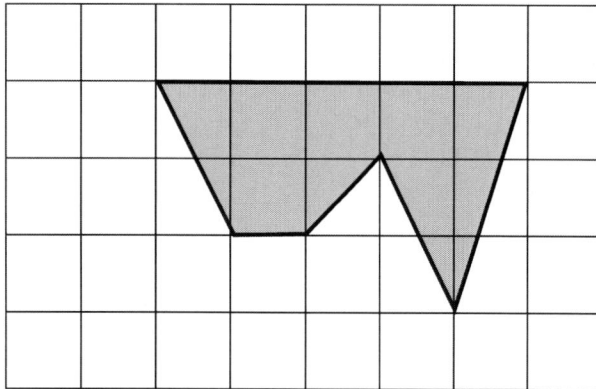

1 square = 1 cm²

| cm² |

1 mark

12. This cuboid is made from 1 centimetre cubes.

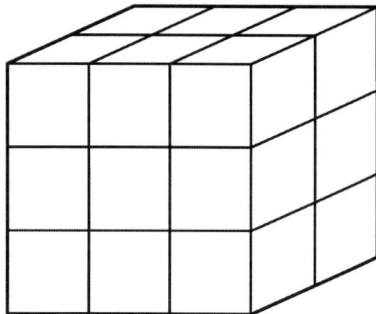

What is the volume of the cuboid in cm³?

| cm³ |

1 mark

13. The world record for running 1500 m is 3 minutes 26 seconds.

How many seconds is this?

| seconds |

1 mark

14. The jug contains 40 ml of water.

I pour in another 35 ml.

Draw an arrow to show the new level of water.

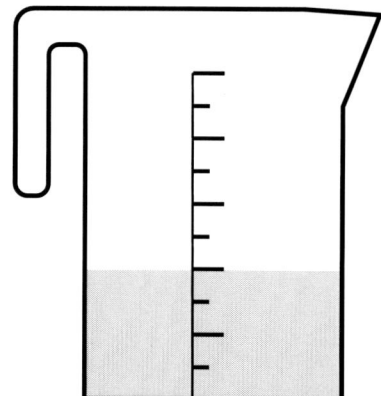

1 mark

/15

Total for this test

Name: _____ Class: _____ Date: _____

---

1. Write the masses in order. Start with the heaviest mass.

1.7 kg   0.25 kg $\frac{3}{4}$ kg   7 kg   700 g

_____

heaviest   **lightest**

1 mark

---

2. Circle the two lengths that are equal.

3 km   0.3 m   30 mm   30 cm

1 mark

---

3. Use the information in this table to work out how many litres there are in one gallon.

Litres (*l*)		Pints		Gallons
0.56	=	1		
_____	=	8	=	1

1 mark

---

4. An inch is about 2.5 centimetres.

How many inches are there in 1 metre?

inches

1 mark

---

5. This tile pattern is made from three regular hexagons.

The total distance around the edges of one hexagon is 36 cm.

Calculate the perimeter of the pattern.

Show how you work it out.

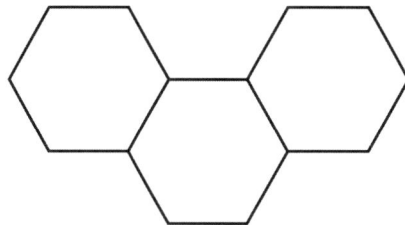

cm

2 marks

Total for this page

6. This grid is made of 1 cm squares.
What is the area of the shaded shape?

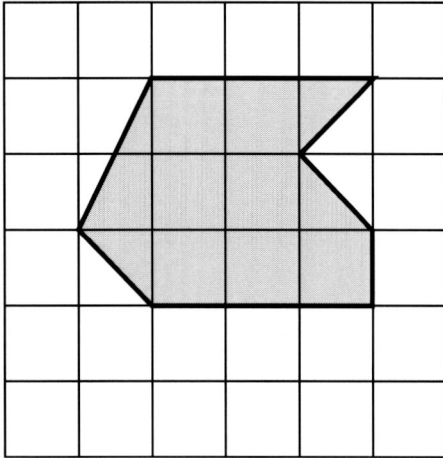

[ ] cm²

[ ]
1 mark

7. The length of a rectangle is 9 cm.

The width is 4 cm.

What is the area of the rectangle?

Include the correct units.

[ ]

[ ]
1 mark

8. A kettle can fill 5 mugs.

Each mug holds 400 millilitres.

How many litres does the kettle hold?

[ ] litres

[ ]
1 mark

9. This cuboid is made from centimetre cubes.

How many centimetre cubes are used to make the cuboid?

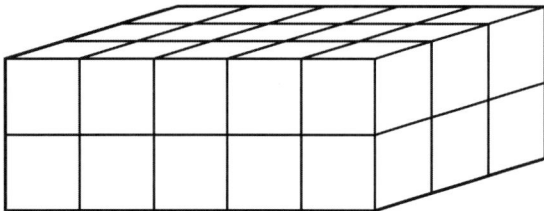

[ ] cm³

[ ]
1 mark

10. A flight from Britain to America takes 8 hours 12 minutes.

How many minutes is this altogether?

_____ minutes

[ ]
1 mark

11. A ferry from Holyhead left at 08:05 and arrived in Dublin at 11:30.

How many minutes did the ferry take?

_____ minutes

[ ]
1 mark

[ ]
Total for
this page

74

12. Two regular octagons are the same size.

They join along one edge to make a new shape.

The outer perimeter of the new shape is 1.4 metres.

How many centimetres long is each edge?

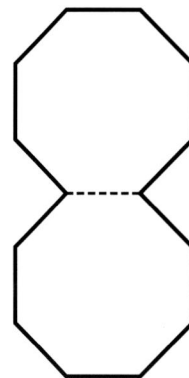

Show your working.

| | cm |

1 mark

---

13. Sam had:

4 rides on the dodgems

2 rides on the big wheel

and 3 rides on the roller coaster.

Fairground rides	
Dodgems	£1.85
Big wheel	£2.35
Roller coaster	£2.90

How much did he pay altogether?   £

2 marks

1 mark

/15

Total for this test

Name: _____ Class: _____ Date: _____

1. Write in the missing numbers.

0.6 metres = [   ] centimetres

0.6 metres = [   ] millimetres

1 mark

2. Jan needs $\frac{2}{5}$ of a litre of milk.

Draw a line across the jug to show $\frac{2}{5}$ of a litre.

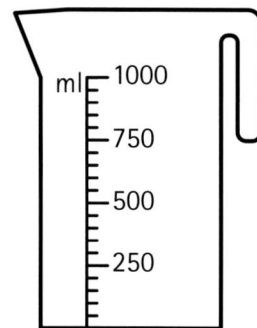

ml ┌ 1000
   ├ 750
   ├ 500
   ├ 250

1 mark

3. A kilogram is about 2.2 pounds.

Jak needs to buy $2\frac{1}{2}$ kg of potatoes.

Using this estimation, how many pounds of potatoes does Jak buy?

[   ] pounds

1 mark

4. Use the information in this table to work out how many centimetres there are in one yard.

Centimetres (cm)		Inches		Yards
2.5	=	1		
_____	=	36	=	1

1 mark

[ ] Total for this page

5. What is the perimeter of the shaded shape?

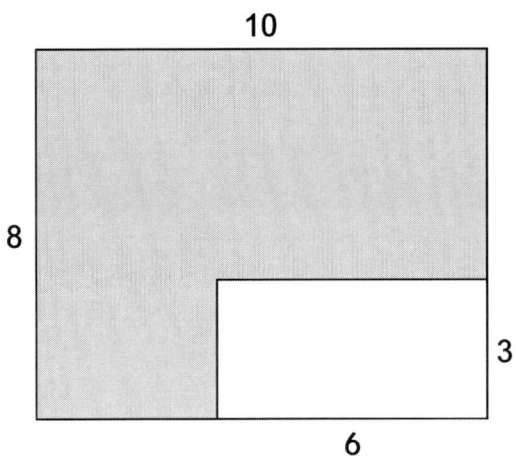

cm	
	1 mark

6. This shape is drawn on centimetre-squared paper.

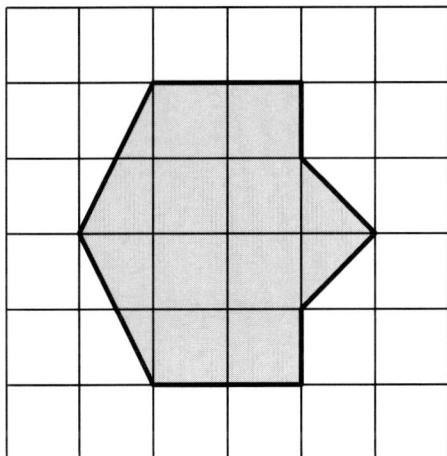

cm²	
	1 mark

Total for this page

7. These shapes are drawn on centimetre squared paper.

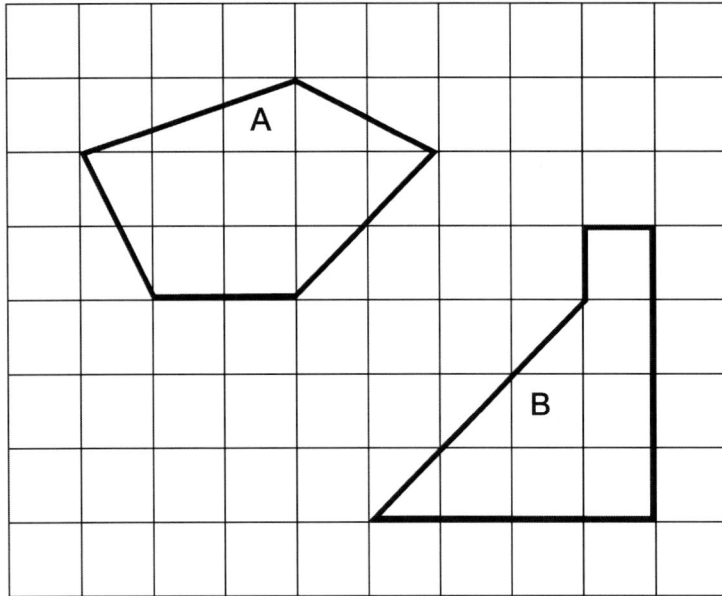

Work out the area of each shape. **A** [ ] cm² **B** [ ] cm²

What is the difference between the area of the two shapes? [ ] cm²

[ ]
2 marks

8. Tara has a 2 *l* bottle of lemonade.

She has 7 glasses which can be almost filled with the lemonade.

If she uses all the lemonade, give an estimate of the capacity of the glass.

[ ] ml

[ ]
1 mark

9. This cuboid is made from centimetre cubes.

How many centimetre cubes are used to make the cuboid?

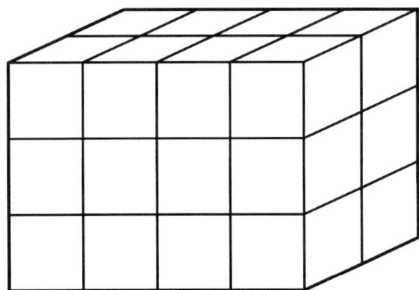

[ ] cm³

[ ]
1 mark

[ ]
Total for
this page

10. How many seconds are in 5 minutes?

| seconds |

1 mark

11. An advert says 'Hire this car for 72 hours.'

How many days is this?

| days |

1 mark

12. A length of string measures 10 m.

Rob cuts off six pieces. Each piece measures 120 cm.

How much string is left over?

Show how you work it out.

1 mark

13.

Price list		
footballs	⚽	£4.40 each
tennis balls		£6.50 for 3
golf balls		£4.35 for 4

I buy 8 golf balls, 12 tennis balls and 2 footballs.

How much change will I get from £50?

£

2 marks

/15

Total for this test

Year 5
Measurement Test 4(H)

Name: _____ Class: _____ Date: _____

---

1. Write these lengths in order from shortest to longest.

2.05 m   2.5 cm   250 cm   20 mm

_____

shortest   **longest**

---

2. This grid is made of 1 cm squares.

What is the area of the shaded shape?

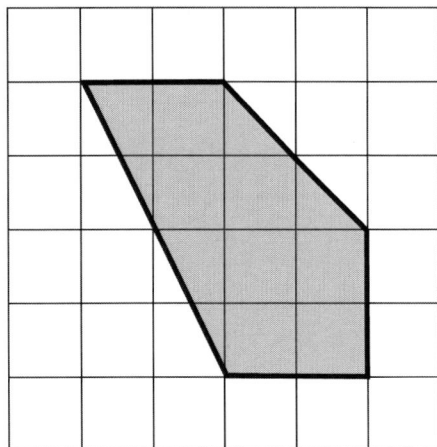

cm²

---

3. Lola buys two muesli bars and a quarter kilogram of nuts.

How much change does she get from £5?

Muesli bar	55p
1 kg of nuts	£2.20

£

4. Joe is 1.52 m tall.

Alice is 1.36 m tall.

How much taller is Joe than Alice?

	cm

1 mark

5. What is the perimeter of this shape?

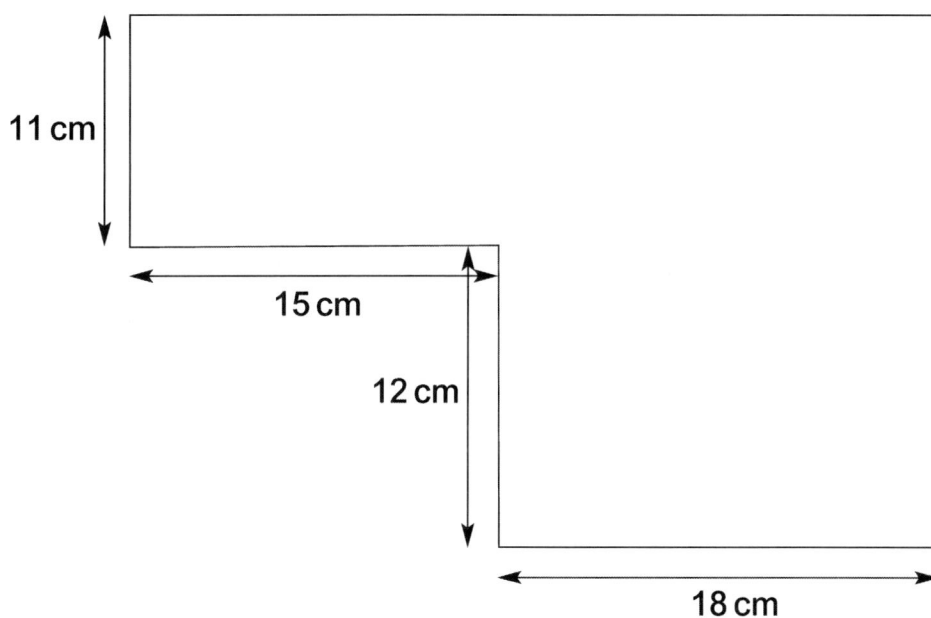

11 cm

15 cm

12 cm

18 cm

	cm

2 marks

6. Circle the number of seconds in one hour.

120 seconds   300 seconds   360 seconds

3000 seconds   3600 seconds

1 mark

Total for
this page

81

7. Write these lengths in order, smallest first.

5.5 m   450 mm   5 200 mm   42 cm   0.006 km

_____

smallest   **longest**

☐ 1 mark

8. Convert 0.05 kg to grams.

| grams |

☐ 1 mark

9. Convert 200 miles to kilometres.

| kilometres |

☐ 1 mark

10. Sian uses some metre squares to make a rectangle.

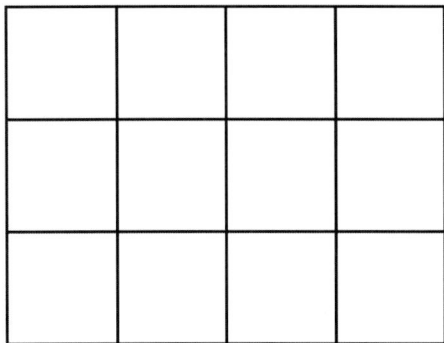

She then rearranges the squares to make a different rectangle.

What could the perimeter of this rectangle be?

| m |

☐ 1 mark

11. Sian uses some other metre squares to make a rectangle with a perimeter of 20 m.

What could its area be?

| m² |

☐ 1 mark

12. What is the area of this triangle?

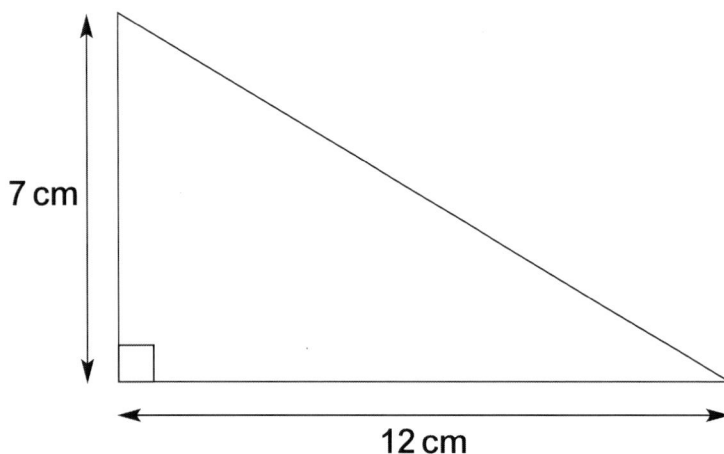

7 cm

12 cm

| cm² |

☐ 1 mark

☐ Total for this page

13. A cuboid is 6 cm long, 4 cm wide and 5 cm high.
What is the volume of the cuboid?

cm³

1 mark

14. What is the area of this parallelogram?

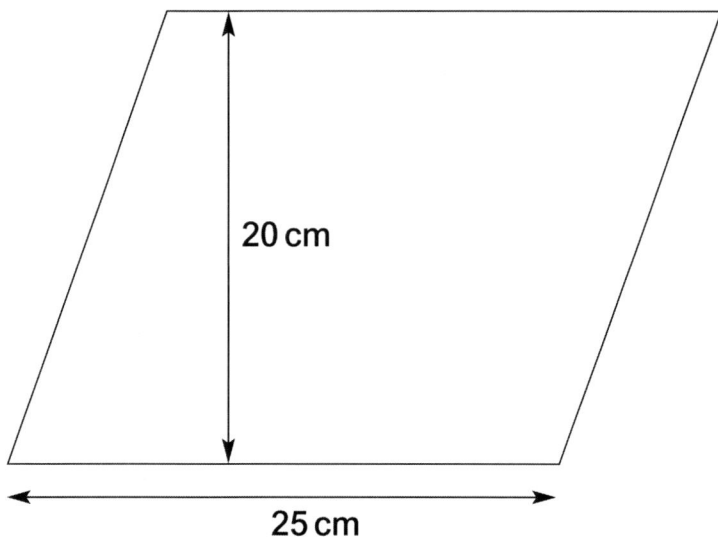

20 cm

25 cm

cm²

1 mark

/15

**Total for
this test**

Year 5
Measurement Test 5: Mental mathematics

Instructions – to be read to pupils

Listen carefully to these instructions. I am going to ask you 20 questions. I will read each question twice. Listen carefully both times. You will then have time to work out your answer.

On your sheet there is an answer box for each question. Some questions are easy and some are harder. For some questions, important information is already written down for you on the sheet.

Work out the answer to each question in your head. Don't try to write down your calculations as this wastes time and you may miss the next question. If it helps you, you may jot things down outside the answer box.

If you can't work out an answer, put a cross in the answer box. If you make a mistake, cross out the wrong answer and then write the correct answer next to it.

You won't be able to ask questions once the test has begun. If you have any questions you may ask them now.

Now we are ready to start the test.

		Mark	Answer

For these questions, you will have 5 seconds to work out each answer and write it down.

		Mark	Answer
1.	Change 8 kilometres to metres.	1	8000
2.	A film lasts 2 hours. How many minutes is this?	1	120
3.	Change 8:00 p.m. to 24-hour time.	1	20:00
4.	How many millilitres are there in 7 litres?	1	7000
5.	How many grams are there in 7 kilograms?	1	7000

For these questions, you will have 10 seconds to work out each answer and write it down.

		Mark	Answer
6.	One side of a square is 12 centimetres. What is the perimeter of the square?	1	48
7.	Beth spends 12 pounds, 50 pence. How much change would she get from 20 pounds?	1	7.50
8.	Look at your answer sheet. What is the perimeter of the rectangle?	1	30
9.	A bucket holds five and a half litres. How many millilitres is this?	1	5500
10.	Look at your answer sheet. A parcel weighs 500 grams. Circle how much the parcel weighs in kilograms.	1	0.5 kg
11.	A rectangle is 8 centimetres long and 4 centimetres wide. What is the area of the rectangle?	1	32
12.	Look at your answer sheet. The cube is made from centimetre cubes. How many centimetre cubes have been used to make the larger cube?	1	8
13.	The area of a square is 64 metres squared. What is the length of one side?	1	8
14.	Mira weighs a cake. It weighs 1.05 kilograms. How many grams is this?	1	1050
15.	The area of a parallelogram is 24 centimetres squared. The parallelogram is 8 centimetres long. What is the height of the parallelogram?	1	3

For these questions, you will have 15 seconds to work out each answer and write it down.

		Mark	Answer
16.	Euan has two boxes of CDs. One weighs 700 grams and the other weighs 1.5 kilograms. What is the total mass of his boxes of CDs in kilograms?	1	Accept 2.2
17.	A jug contains 1 litre of water. I pour out 40 millilitres. How much is left in the jug?	1	960
18.	Look at your answer sheet. Circle the approximate equivalent of 20 miles in kilometres.	1	32 km
19.	The area of a triangle is 20 centimetres squared. The base of the triangle is 10 centimetres. How high is the triangle?	1	4
20.	Look at your answer sheet. The cube is a 1 centimetre cube. What is the volume in millimetre cubes?	1	1000

Now put down your pen or pencil. The test is finished.

Year 5
Measurement

Test 5: Mental mathematics

Name: _____ Class: _____ Date: _____

5-second questions

1.		m

2.		minutes

3.		

4.		ml

5.		g

10-second questions

6.		cm	12 cm

7.	£		£12.50

8.	m	3 m / 12 m

9.		ml

10.	50 kg 0.5 kg 0.05 kg 5.0 kg

11.		cm²

12.	cm³	

13.		m	64 m²

14.		g	1.05 kg

15.		cm	24 cm²

15-second questions

16.		kg

17.		ml	40 ml

18.	5 km 12 km 32 km 100 km

19.		cm

20.	mm³	1 cm / 1 cm / 1 cm

Total for this test
/20

Year 5
Geometry Test 1(L)

Name: _____ Class: _____ Date: _____

1. ✓ the right-angled triangle.

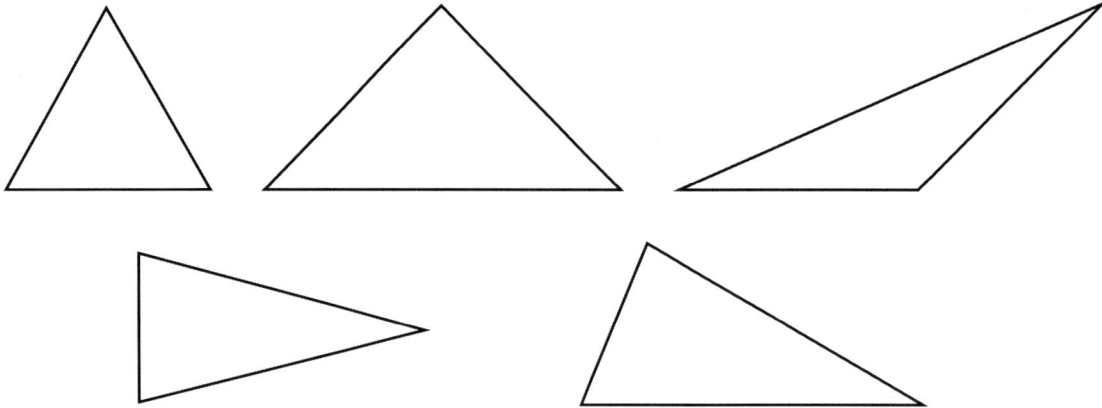

1 mark

2. ✓ the smallest angle.

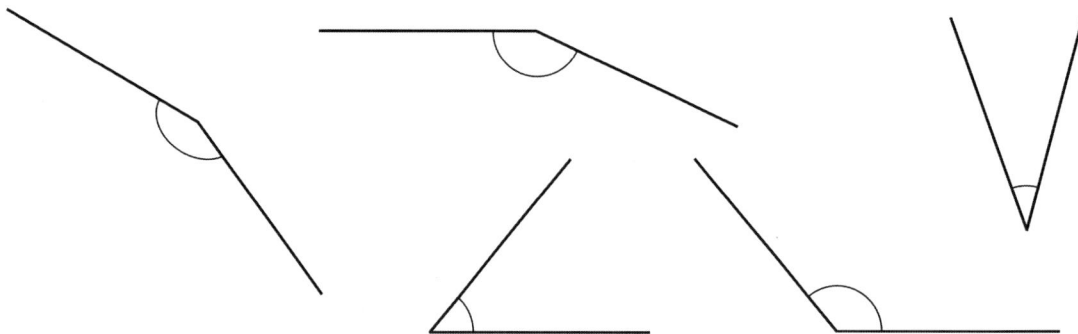

1 mark

3. How many lines of symmetry are there in this square?

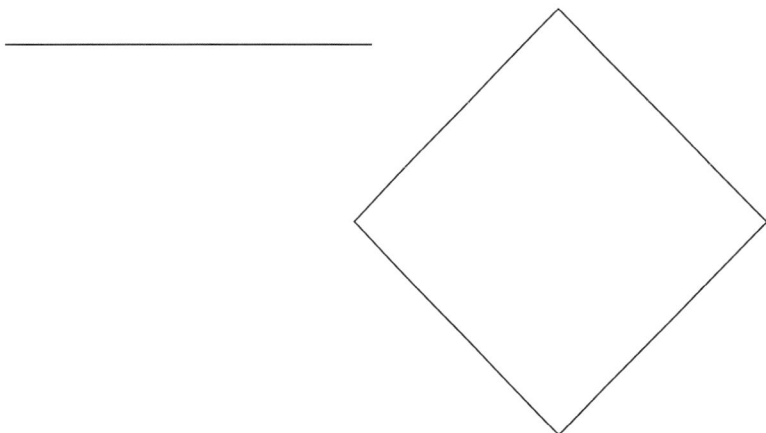

_____

1 mark

Total for
this page

4. Complete this shape to make it symmetrical.

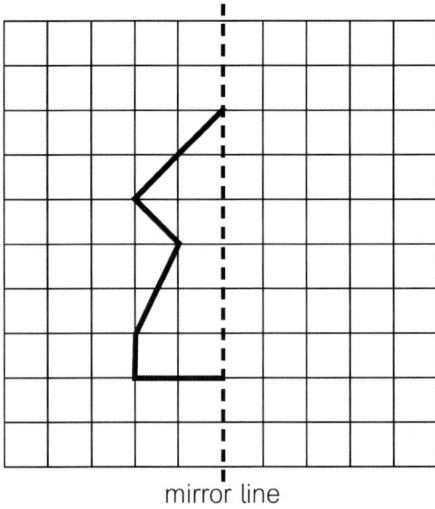

mirror line

1 mark

5. Give the coordinates of the point marked on the grid.

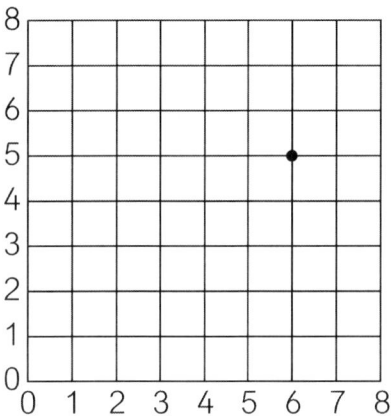

_____

1 mark

6. Triangle A has been translated to Triangle B.

Describe the translation.

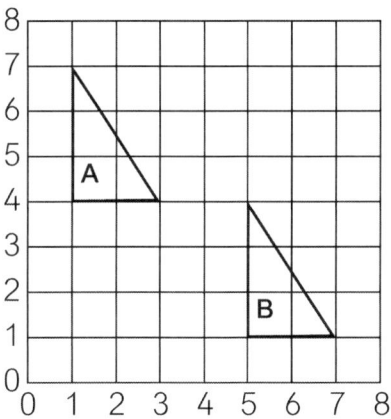

_____

1 mark

Total for
this page

7. Two sides of a square have been drawn on this grid.

Three of the vertices can be seen.

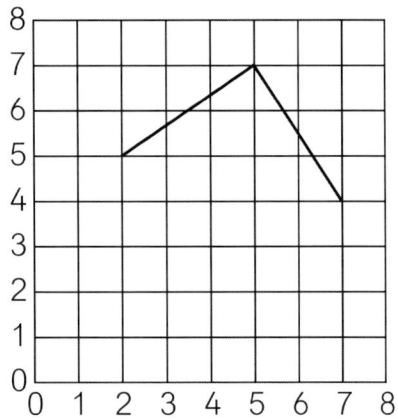

What are the coordinates of the fourth vertex?

_____

1 mark

8. This is the net of a 3-D shape.

Name the shape.

_____

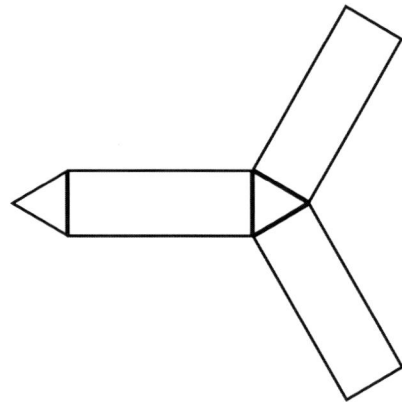

1 mark

9. Reflect the shape in the mirror line.

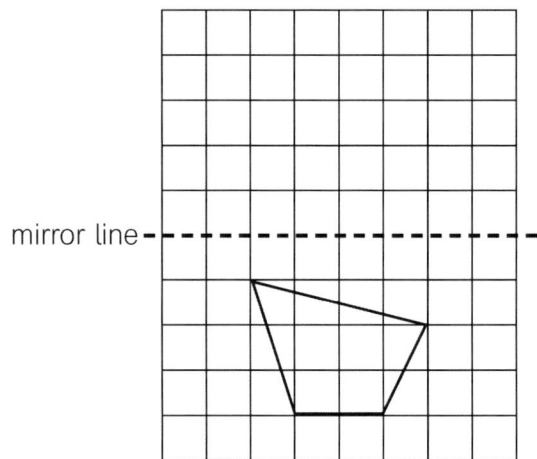

mirror line

1 mark

10. Measure angle x accurately.

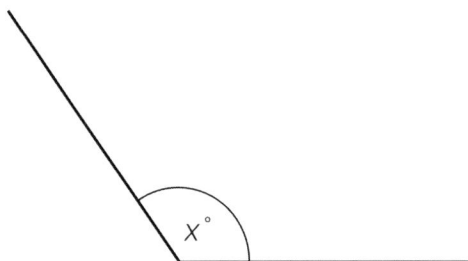

1 mark

 °

Total for this page

11. ✓ all the regular shapes.

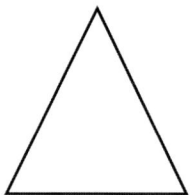

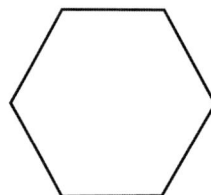

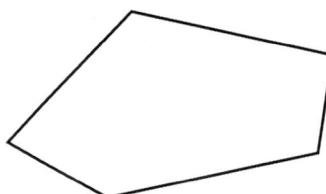

1 mark

12. Estimate the size of the marked angle.

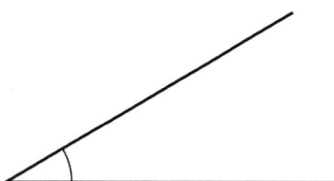

°

1 mark

13. Draw an angle of 70°.

1 mark

14. Calculate the size of the angle marked x.

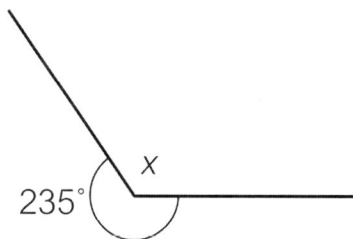

235°   x

°

1 mark

15. The area of this rectangle is 240 cm².
Calculate the length of the rectangle.

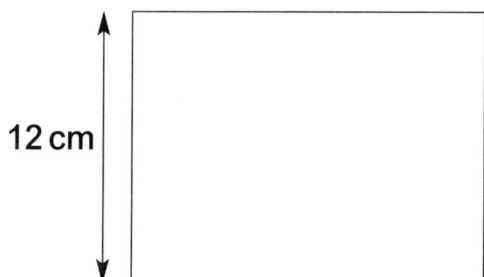

12 cm

cm

1 mark

/15

**Total for
this test**

Name: _____ Class: _____ Date: _____

1. Reflect the shape in the mirror line.

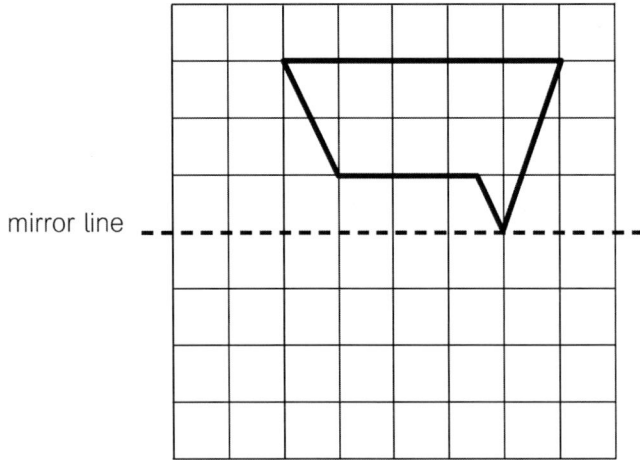

mirror line

1 mark

2. This is a net.

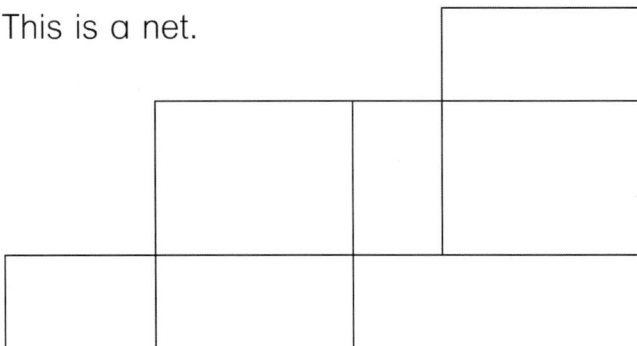

Name the 3-D shape.

_____

1 mark

3. Estimate the size of the marked angle.

°

1 mark

4. Draw an angle of 135°.

1 mark

Total for this page

5. Calculate the angle marked y.

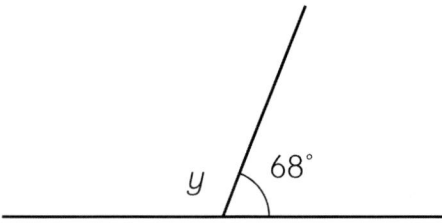

	°

1 mark

6. Calculate the angle marked v.

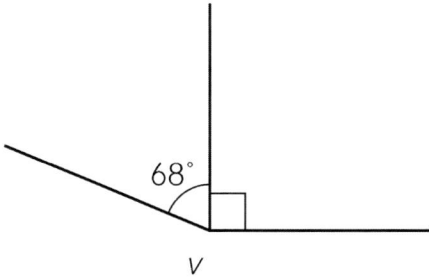

	°

1 mark

7. The perimeter of a rectangle is 90 cm.
The length of the rectangle is 27 cm.
What is the width of the rectangle?

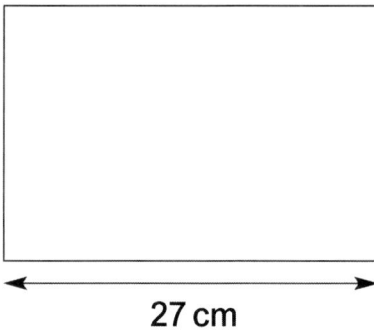

27 cm

	cm

2 marks

8. This shape is a rectangle.
A diagonal has been drawn.

Calculate the missing angles s and t.

$s =$ ☐ ° $t =$ ☐ °

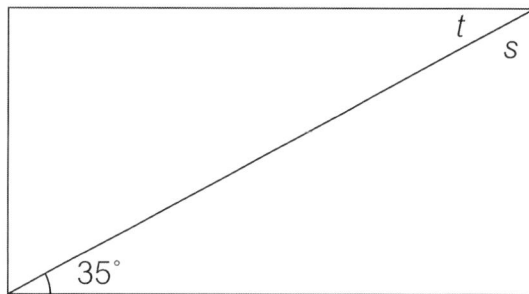

2 marks

☐
Total for
this page

9. ✓ the regular shape.

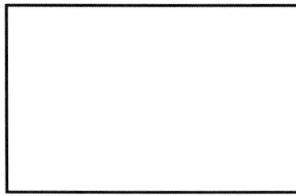

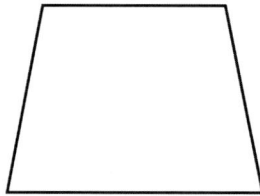

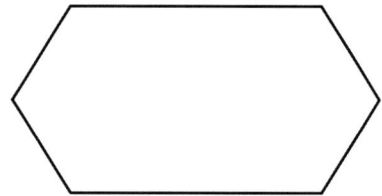

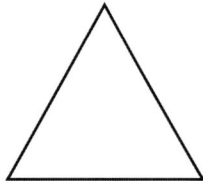

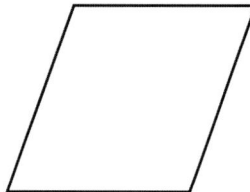

1 mark

10. Translate the triangle so that point A moves to point B.

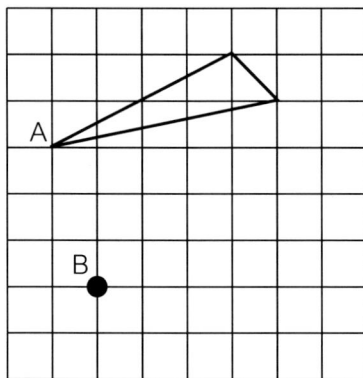

1 mark

11. Explain why this shape is irregular.

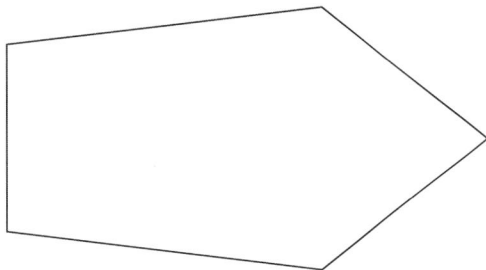

_____

_____

1 mark

Total for
this page

12. These five lines meet at a point, making five equal angles.

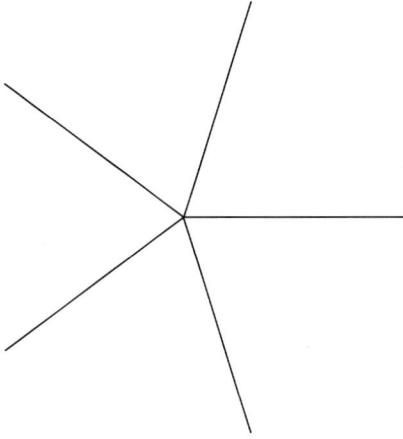

Calculate the value of the angles.

	°

1 mark

13. A square has a perimeter of 64 cm.
How long is each side?

	cm

1 mark

/15

**Total for
this test**

Name: _____ Class: _____ Date: _____

1. This is the net of a 3-D shape.
Name the shape.

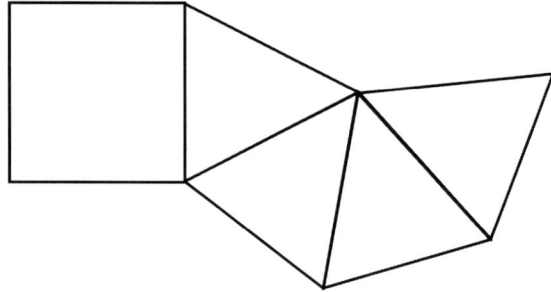

_____

1 mark

2. Name this 3-D shape.

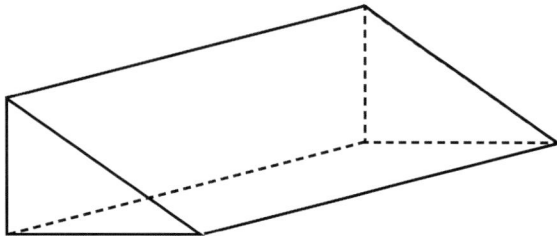

_____

1 mark

3. Translate the rectangle so point A moves to point B.

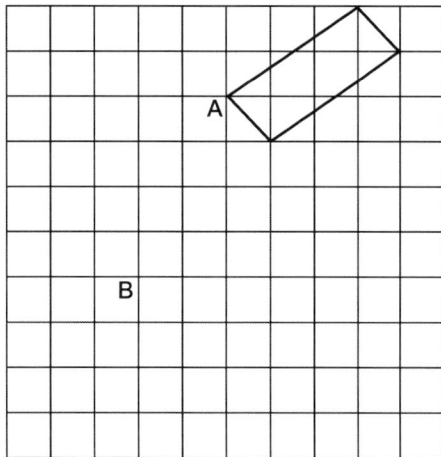

1 mark

4. Put these angle names in order of size, smallest first.

obtuse   acute   reflex   right

_____

1 mark

Total for
this page

5.

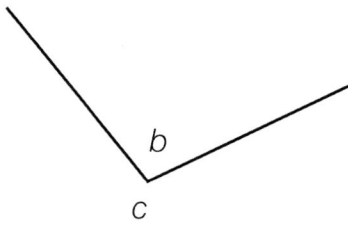

a) Measure angle b.

$b = $ [   ] °

1 mark

b) Use your answer to calculate angle c.

$c = $ [   ] °

1 mark

6. Draw an angle of 145°.

1 mark

7. A right angle is marked between two lines.

Calculate the size of the angle marked a.

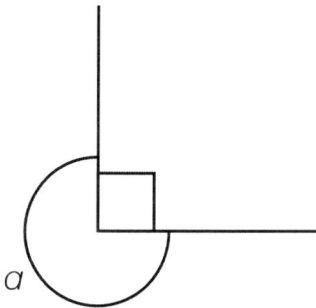

$a = $ [   ] °

1 mark

8. Reflect the shape in the vertical mirror line, and then reflect this new shape in the horizontal mirror line.

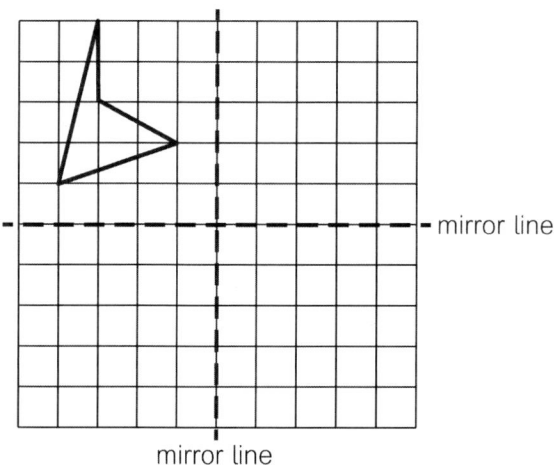

mirror line

mirror line

2 marks

Total for this page

9. The angles marked a are all equal.

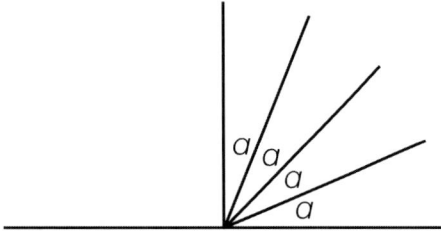

What is the size of a ?

$a =$ ⬚ ° ☐

1 mark

10. Calculate the angle marked d in this square.

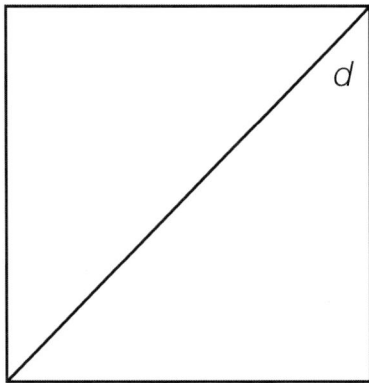

$d =$ ⬚ ° ☐

1 mark

11. ✓ the irregular shape.

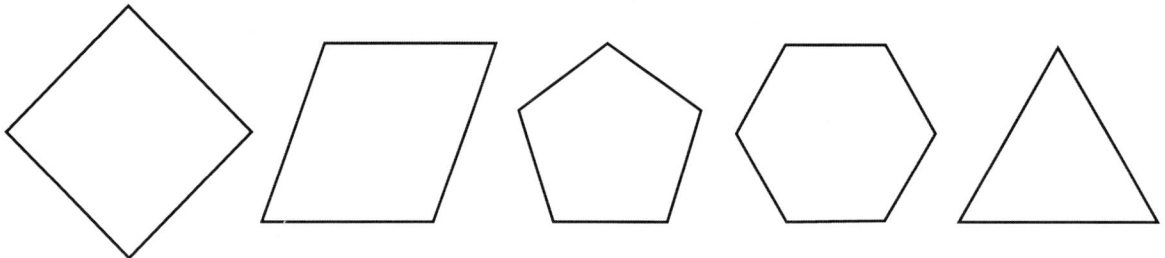

☐

1 mark

12. A regular octagon has a perimeter of 40 cm.

What is the length of one side of the octagon?

⬚ cm ☐

1 mark

13. This shape is a rectangle.

The diagonal is 30 cm.

Find the length of the line marked n.

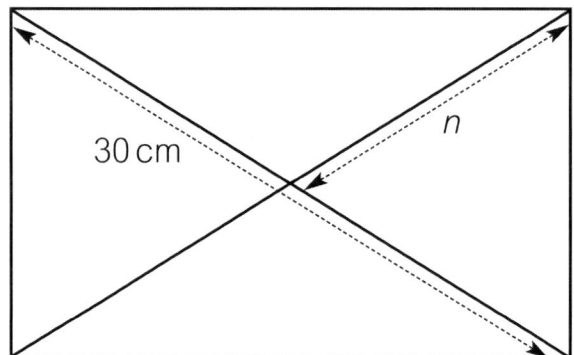

30 cm

$n =$ ⬚ cm

☐

1 mark

/15

Total for this test

Year 5
Geometry Test 4(H)

1. Reflect the shape in the mirror line.

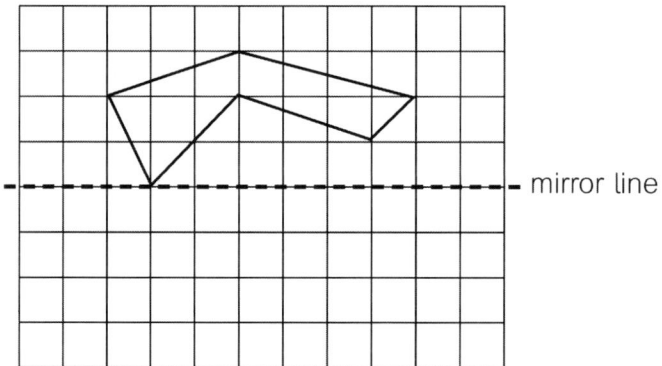

— mirror line

1 mark

2. This is the net of a 3-D shape.

Name the shape.

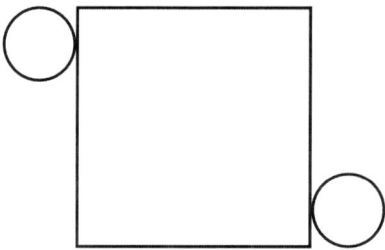

_____

1 mark

3. Put these angles in order, largest first.

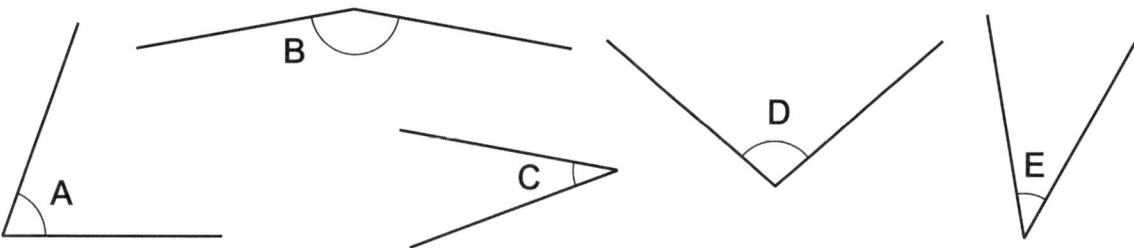

Write the letters for each angle.

_____

1 mark

Total for
this page

4.   Draw an angle of 165°.

1 mark

---

5.   Calculate the size of the angle m.

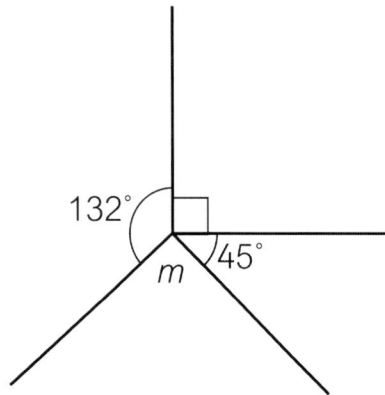

$132°$ $45°$ m

$$m = \boxed{} °$$

1 mark

---

6.   Calculate the size of angle n.

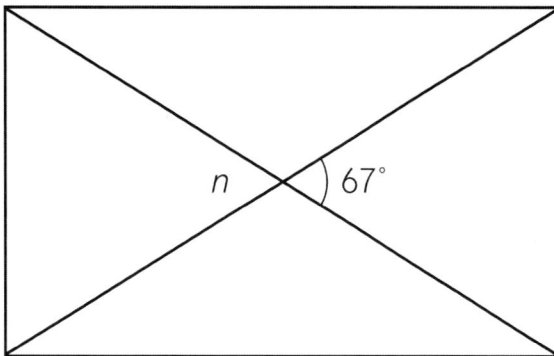

n $67°$

$$n = \boxed{} °$$

1 mark

---

7.   ✓ the correct statement about a regular shape.

☐   The rectangle has a length of 10 cm and a width of 9 cm.

☐   The pentagon has five sides, each 1 cm longer than the other.

☐   The hexagon has 6 angles; each one is 120°.

1 mark

☐   The octagon has a perimeter of 40 cm; only one side is 5 cm.

Total for
this page

8. Here is part of a triangle.

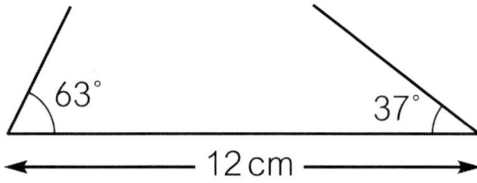

63° 37° 12 cm

Copy and complete the triangle using a ruler and angle measurer.

1 mark

9. This cuboid is made from centimetre cubes.

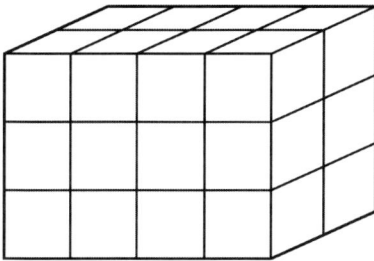

Part of the net of this cuboid is drawn on the squared paper.

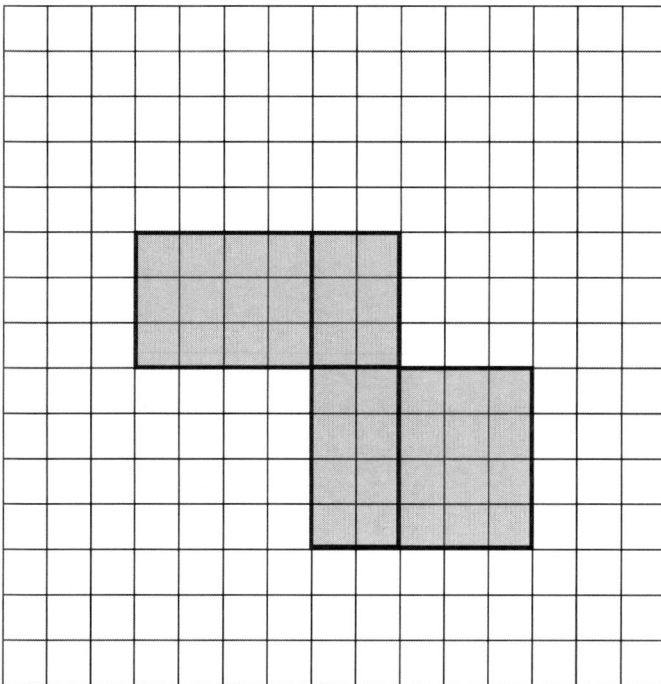

Complete the net of the cuboid.

1 mark

Total for this page

10. Find the missing angles in these triangles.

a)

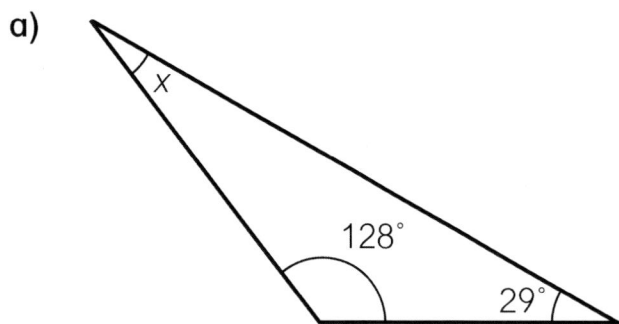

$x =$ [ ]°   [ ]
1 mark

b)

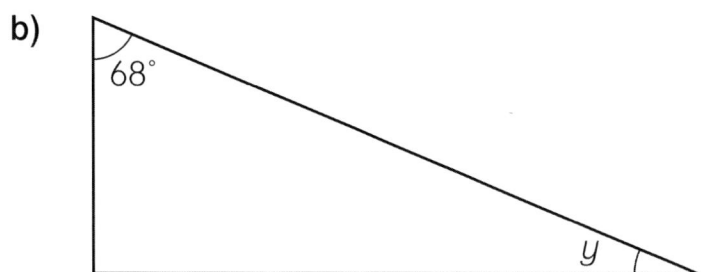

$y =$ [ ]°   [ ]
1 mark

11. The radius of a circle is 24 cm.

What is the diameter of the circle?

[ ] cm   [ ]
1 mark

12. Here are three circles.

Name the parts of the circle shown by the dotted lines.

A 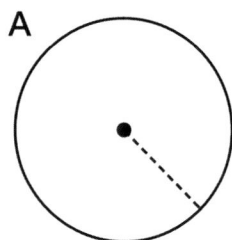   B 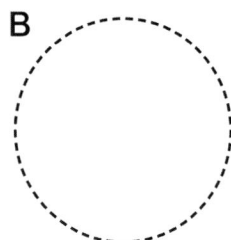   C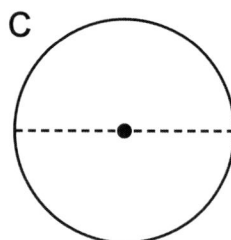

A = _____

B = _____

C = _____

[ ]
2 marks

13. Calculate the missing angles.

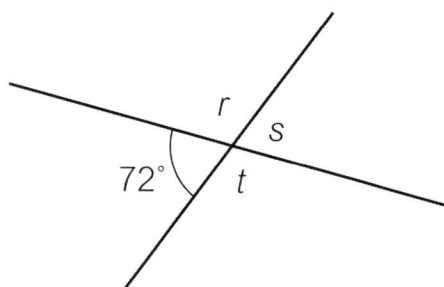

$r =$ [ ]°

$s =$ [ ]°

$t =$ [ ]°   [ ]
1 mark

[ ] /15

Total for this test

100

Year 5
Geometry   Test 5: Mental mathematics

Instructions – to be read to pupils

Listen carefully to these instructions. I am going to ask you 20 questions. I will read each question twice. Listen carefully both times. You will then have time to work out your answer.

On your sheet there is an answer box for each question. Some questions are easy and some are harder. For some questions, important information is already written down for you on the sheet.

Work out the answer to each question in your head. Don't try to write down your calculations as this wastes time and you may miss the next question. If it helps you, you may jot things down outside the answer box.

If you can't work out an answer, put a cross in the answer box. If you make a mistake, cross out the wrong answer and then write the correct answer next to it.

You won't be able to ask questions once the test has begun. If you have any questions you may ask them now.

Now we are ready to start the test.

		Mark	Answer

For these questions, you will have 5 seconds to work out each answer and write it down.

		Mark	Answer
1.	Look at your answer sheet. Circle the shape that is not a quadrilateral.	1	Decagon circled
2.	How many degrees in a whole turn?	1	360
3.	Look at your answer sheet. Which line is a line of symmetry?	1	C
4.	Look at your answer sheet. What are the coordinates of the point x?	1	(3, 2)
5.	Two angles make a right angle. One of the angles is 30 degrees. What is the size of the other angle?	1	60

For these questions, you will have 10 seconds to work out each answer and write it down.

		Mark	Answer
6.	Two angles make a straight line. One of the angles is 50 degrees. What is the other angle?	1	130°
7.	What fraction of a whole turn is 270 degrees?	1	$\frac{3}{4}$, accept 0.75, 75%
8.	Look at your answer sheet. Estimate the size of angle x.	1	60 (accept answers between 50–70 inclusive)
9.	Look at your answer sheet. Circle all the shapes that show a line of symmetry.	1	1st, 2nd and 4th shapes circled or otherwise indicated.
10.	Name the 3-D shape that has 6 faces; each face is a square.	1	Cube
11.	How many degrees are there in two right angles?	1	180
12.	When a shape is translated 5 units right and 2 units up, does the shape: A: get bigger? B: stay the same size? C: get smaller?	1	B
13.	Look at your answer sheet. Name the 3-D shape made from this net.	1	Triangular prism
14.	Name the quadrilateral that has only one pair of parallel lines.	1	Trapezoid/Trapezium
15.	Look at your answer sheet. Circle the name of the outside line around a circle.	1	Circumference

For these questions, you will have 15 seconds to work out each answer and write it down.

		Mark	Answer
16.	Three identical angles meet at a point. What is the size of each angle?	1	120
17.	A regular hexagon has a side length of 7 centimetres. What is its perimeter?	1	42
18.	The perimeter of a rectangle is 24 centimetres. The length of the rectangle is 8 centimetres. How wide is the rectangle?	1	4
19.	Two angles in a triangle are 40 degrees and 65 degrees. What is the size of the third angle?	1	75
20.	Look at your answer sheet. Circle the number of lines of symmetry in a rectangle.	1	2 circled

Now put down your pen or pencil. The test is finished.

Year 5
Geometry
Test 5: Mental mathematics

Name: _____ Class: _____ Date: _____

5-second questions

1.	kite rhombus square decagon parallelogram

2.	°

3.	

4.	(,)	

5.	°

10-second questions

6.	

7.	°

8.	°	

9.	

10.	

11.	°

12.	

13.		

14.	

15.	diameter radius area circumference diagonal

15-second questions

16.	°

17.	cm

18.	cm	24 cm

19.	°	40° 65°

20.	0 2 3 4 8

Total for this test
/20

Year 5
Statistics   Test 1(L)

Name: _____ Class: _____ Date: _____

1. This graph shows the results of a school sports day.

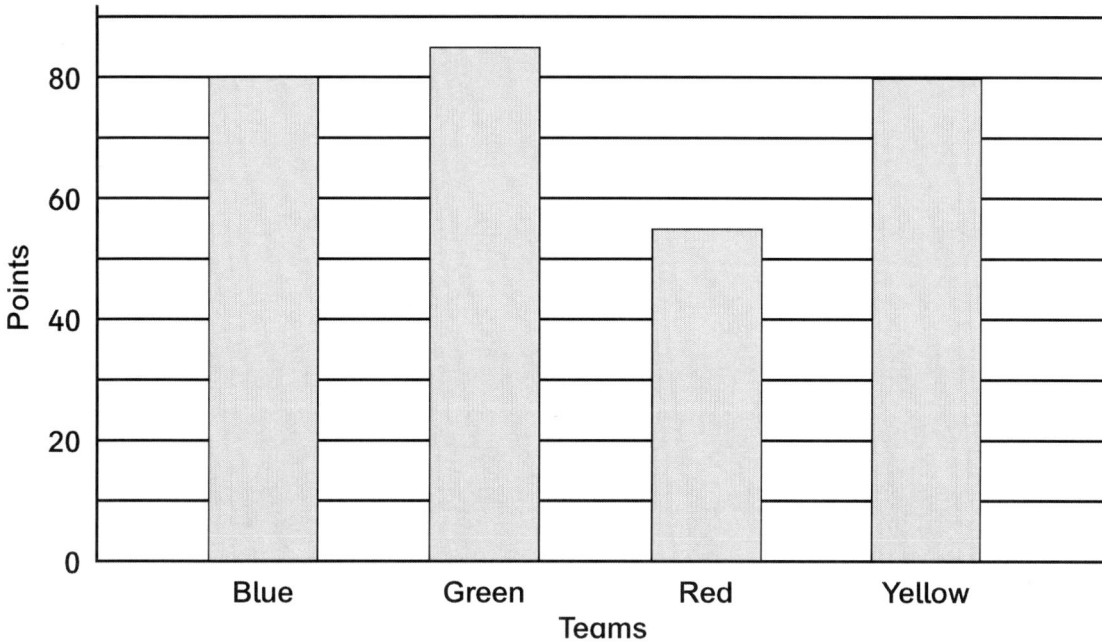

Answer these questions.

a) Estimate the points difference between the team that came first and the team that came fourth?

_____

b) Estimate the total points scored.

_____

1 mark

1 mark

Total for this page

2. Some seeds were planted on Monday.

This graph shows the growth of the seeds.

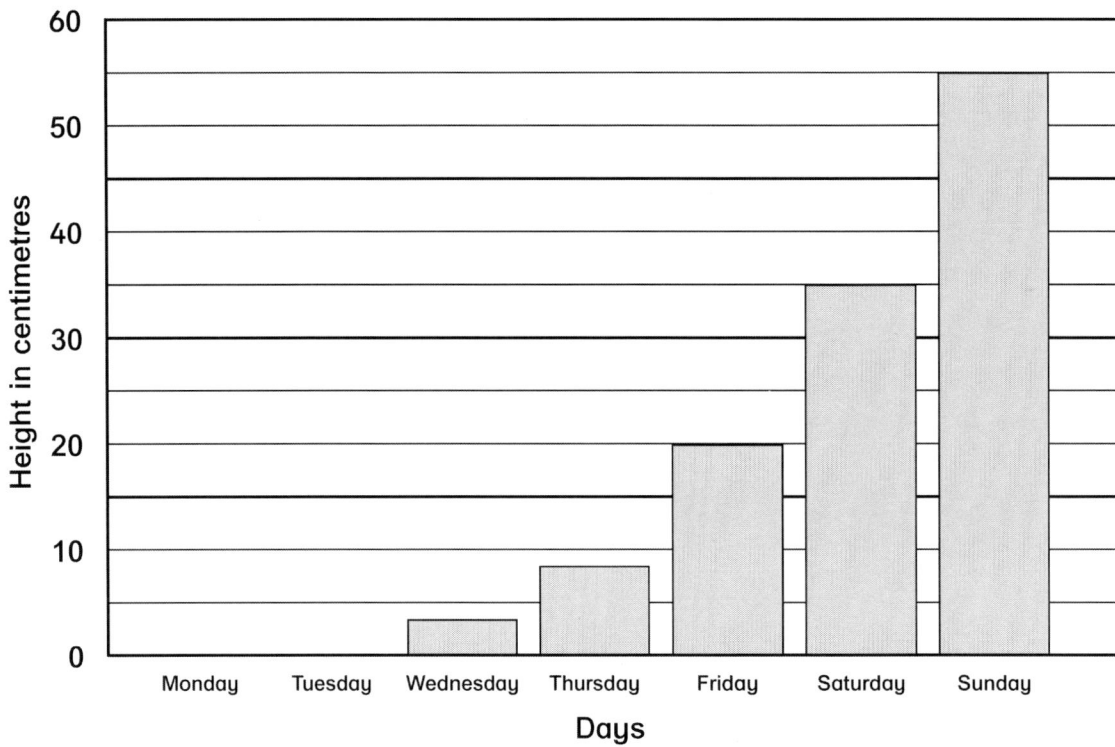

Answer these questions.

a) Between which two days did the seeds grow the most?

_____ to _____

1 mark

b) How tall were the seedlings on Sunday?

_____ cm

1 mark

c) Estimate the height of the seedlings on Thursday?

_____ cm

1 mark

Total for
this page

3. This pictogram shows the number of books read by some children each term.

Panther Group	
Cheetah Group	
Jaguar Group	
Tiger Group	
Lion Group	

Books read ▭ stands for 2 books

Answer these questions.

a) How many books did the Panther Group read? _____

1 mark

b) How many more books did the Tiger Group read than the Lion Group?

_____

1 mark

4. This graph shows the temperature in a classroom through a day.

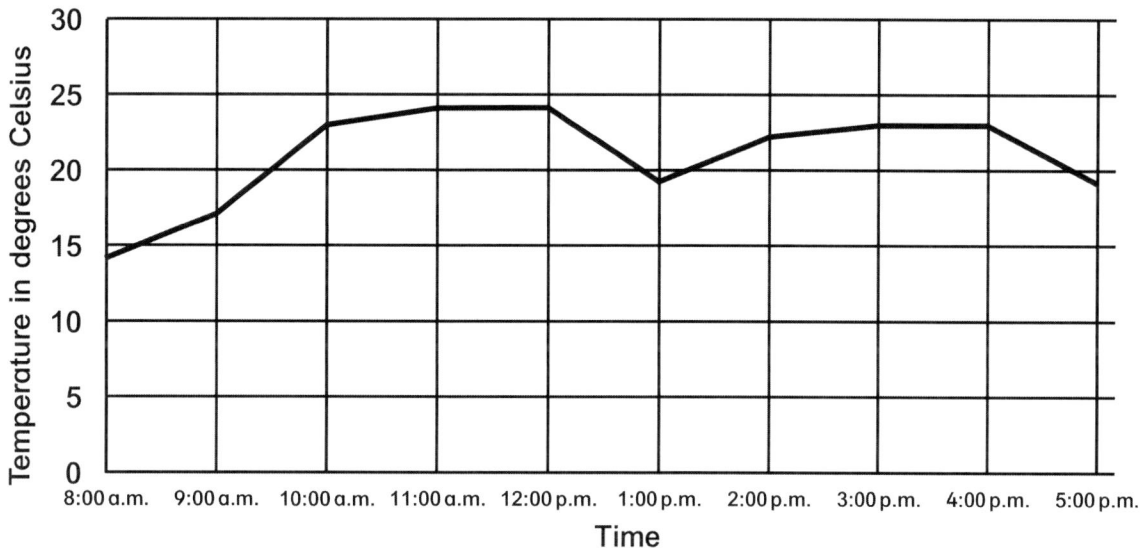

Answer these questions.

a) When was the temperature at its highest?

_____ to _____

1 mark

b) What was the difference between the temperature at 9:00 a.m. and 3:00 p.m.?

_____ °C

1 mark

1 mark

c) Give a reason why the temperature went down after 12:00p.m.

_____

Total for this page

5. This is part of a bus timetable.

	45	48	52	57
Meadow Lane	07:05	08:12	09:18	10:32
Wood Grove	07:20	08:23	09:24	10:46
Valley Hill	07:35	08:36	09:38	10:59
Croft View	07:55	08:51	09:50	11:18
Church Street	08:10	09:06	10:06	11:31
Mill Lane	08:15	09:10	10:12	11:36

Answer these questions.

a) How long does Bus Number 48 take to go from Wood Grove to Church Street?

_____ minutes

1 mark

b) How long does Bus Number 52 take to go from Valley Hill to Mill Lane?

_____ minutes

1 mark

c) Sally needs to arrive at Mill Lane by 10 o'clock.
Which bus would be best to catch?

_____

1 mark

6. Children in a school were given a choice of P.E. activities.
The table shows the numbers of girls and boys and their choices.

	Football	Basketball	Gymnastics	Swimming
Girls	11	14	24	15
Boys	23	12	11	18

Answer these questions.

a) How many boys are there?

_____

1 mark

b) How many children did **not** go swimming?

_____

1 mark

/15

Total for this test

106

Year 5
Statistics   Test 2(M)

Name: _____ Class: _____ Date: _____

1. This graph shows the amount of money in the school fund on the first day of each month.

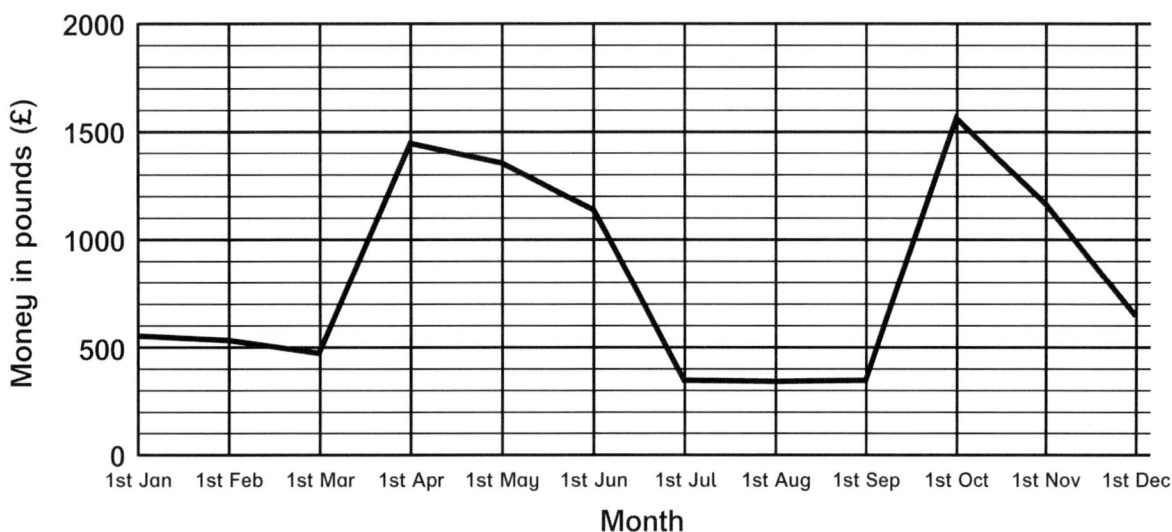

Answer these questions.

a) Estimate the highest amount that was in the school fund.   £ [____]

1 mark

b) The school held two fundraising events.

During which months do you think the school held its fund raising events?

_____ and _____

1 mark

c) During July and August the line is horizontal.

Explain what this means.

_____

_____

1 mark

d) The head teacher, Mrs Jones, said: 'Some money was donated to the school in November.'

Explain how it is possible that the line went down during November.

_____

_____

1 mark

_____

Total for this page

2.   These are the admission prices to Marchwood House.

	Marchwood House Admission Prices		
	House & Garden	House only	Garden only
Adult	£12.75	£9.50	£4.50
Child 5 years – 18 years	£5.75	£4.00	£2.50
Child under 5	£2.00	£2.00	Free
Family Ticket 2 adults + 2 children	£28.00	£22.00	£11.00

Answer these questions.

a) Mr and Mrs Ali and their two children, ages 14 and 12, visit Marchwood House.

They visit the house and gardens.

How much do they save by buying a family ticket?

£ _____

2 marks

b) Mr and Mrs Dunn and their 4-year old daughter visit Marchwood House.

They only visited the house.

How much did it cost them?

£ _____

1 mark

c) A group of 10 adults visits.

5 adults visit the house and garden, the rest only visit the garden.

How much do they pay altogether?

£ _____

1 mark

Total for this page

3.   This graph shows the population of the United Kingdom between 1911 and 2011.

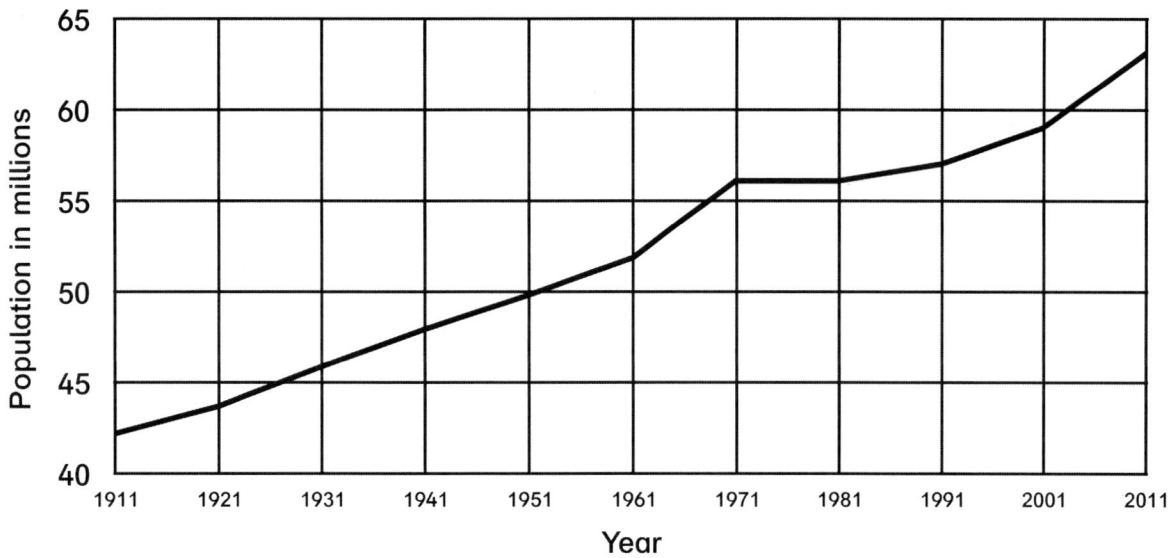

Answer these questions.

a) From 1911 to 1961 the population grew at a steady rate.

Estimate by how many millions the population grew every ten years from 1911 to 1961?

_____

1 mark

b) Between which two years did the population stay roughly the same?

_____ and _____

1 mark

c) Estimate the population of the United Kingdom in 2011.

_____

1 mark

Total for this page

4. This is part of the timetable for trains from London King's Cross to Newcastle.

London King's Cross	12:00	12:30	13:00	13:30	14:00	14:30
Peterborough		13:16		14:16		15:16
Newark		13:44		14:44		15:44
Doncaster		14:10		15:10		16:10
York	13:55	14:35	14:55	15:35	15:55	16:35
Darlington	14:24	15:08	15:24	16:08	16:24	17:08
Durham		15:25		16:25		17:25
Newcastle	14:52	15:42	15:52	16:42	16:52	17:42

Answer these questions.

a) How long does it take the 14:30 train to travel from London King's Cross to Newcastle?

_____

1 mark

b) Use the information in this timetable to estimate when the 15:30 train from London King's Cross will arrive in Newcastle.

_____

1 mark

c) Miss Green arrives at London King's Cross at a quarter to 12.

She wants to catch the next train to Durham.

When will she arrive?

_____

1 mark

d) Mr Jablonsky lives in York.

He walks to the station and gets there at 14:45.

He needs to travel to Durham.

How long will he have to wait for the next train?

_____ minutes

1 mark

/15

Total for this test

Name: _____ Class: _____ Date: _____

1. Mick and Chris completed a maths mental test every two weeks.

They recorded their percentage scores in a graph.

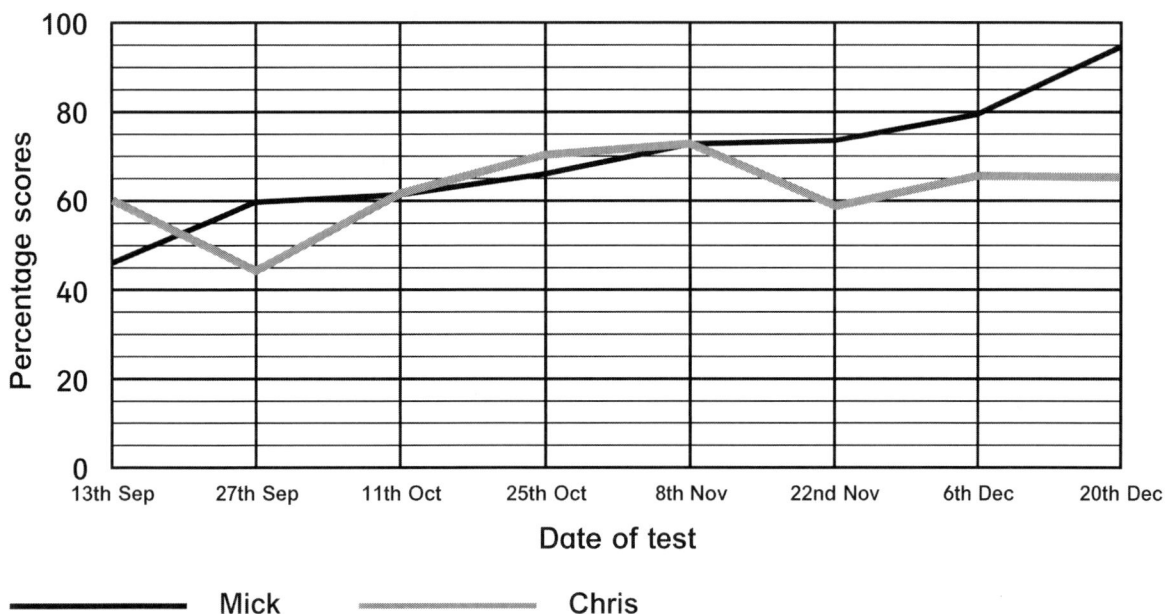

Date of test

——————— Mick   ———————— Chris

Answer these questions.

a) i) Who did better in the first test?

_____

ii) How many more per cent did he score?   [ ] %   [ ]
                                                                         1 mark

b) i) Who did better in the last test?

_____

ii) How many more per cent did he score?   [ ] %   [ ]
                                                                         1 mark

c) What was the lowest score from all the tests?

_____   [ ]
                                                                         1 mark

d) On which dates did Mick and Chris score the same?

_____ and _____   [ ]
                                                                         1 mark

[ ]
Total for
this page

2. This timetable shows an evening's television programmes.

	BBC 1	BBC 2	ITV 1	Channel 4
6:00 p.m.	Pointless Celebrities	Naturewatch	News & Weather	Come Dine With Me
6:30 p.m.			You've Been Framed	News & Weather
7:00 p.m.	Strictly Come Dancing	Horizon		Time Team
7:30 p.m.			The X-Factor	
8:00 p.m.		Film: Robin Hood		Walking Through History
8:30 p.m.	Atlantis			
9:00 p.m.				News & Weather
9:30 p.m.	Casualty			Jeeves and Wooster
10:00 p.m.		Test Match Special	The Jonathan Ross Show	
10:30 p.m.	News & Weather			Film: Clear and Present Danger
11:00 p.m.	Match of the Day			
11:30 p.m.		Politics Today	News & Weather	

Answer these questions.

a) How long is 'The X Factor' on for?

_____

1 mark

b) At the end of 'The X Factor', you change to channel BBC 1.
What would be on BBC 1?

_____

1 mark

c) The film 'Clear and Present Danger' on Channel 4 lasts for 2¼ hours.
At what time did it finish?

_____

1 mark

d) 'Naturewatch' on BBC 2 was on for 2 hours and 20 minutes.
At what time did it start?

_____

1 mark

Total for this page

3. This graph shows the height of boys and girls from the age of 6 years to 18 years.

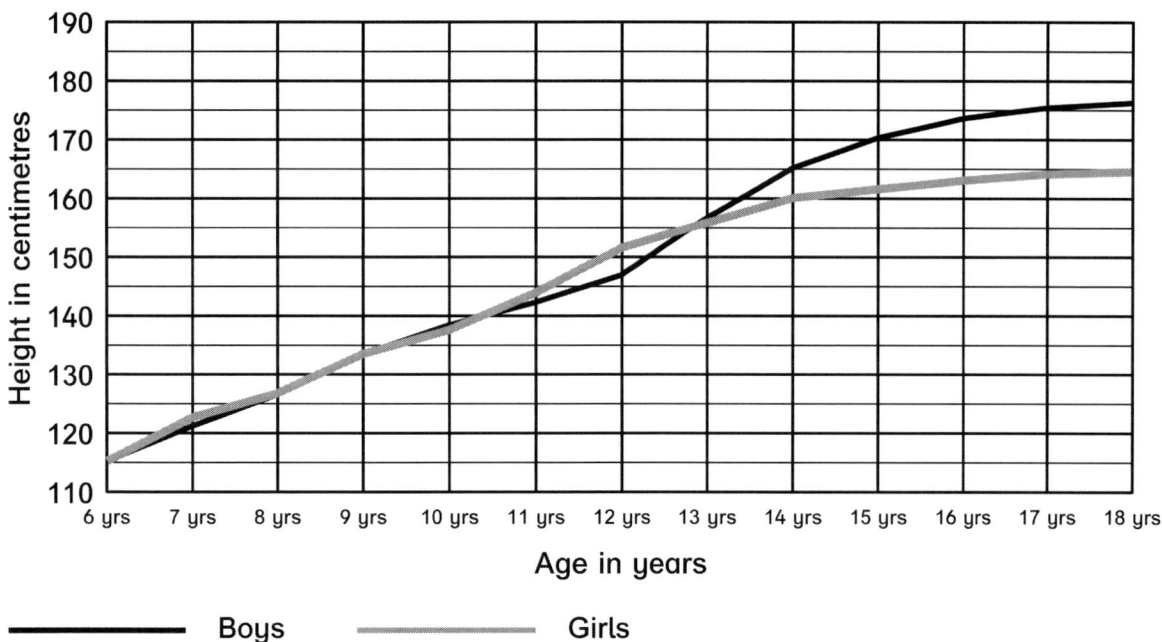

Answer these questions.

a) At what age do girls begin to grow more quickly than boys?

_____

1 mark

b) At what age do boys start to become taller than girls?

_____

1 mark

c) At the age of 18, estimate how much taller boys are than girls.

_____ cm

1 mark

d) At the age of 12, estimate how much taller girls are than boys.

_____ cm

1 mark

Total for this page

4. This timetable shows the times of trains from London Euston to Birmingham New Street.

London Euston	08:03	08:23	08:43	09:03	09:23	09:43	10:03
Watford		08:37			09:37		
Milton Keynes			09:13			10:13	
Rugby	08:51			09:51			10:51
Coventry	09:02	09:22	09:42	10:02	10:22	10:42	11:02
Birmingham International	09:13	09:33	09:53	10:13	10:33	10:53	11:13
Birmingham New Street	09:27	09:45	10:06	10:27	10:45	11:06	11:27

Answer these questions.

a) How long does the 09:43 train from London Euston take to get to Birmingham New Street?

_____

1 mark

b) Galina is in London and must arrive in Milton Keynes by half past ten. What is the latest time she can leave London?

_____

1 mark

c) Ben arrives at London Euston at quarter past eight. How long will he have to wait for a train to Rugby?

_____ minutes

1 mark

/15

Total for this test

Year 5
Statistics   Test 4(H)

1. Mr White runs an ice cream van.

   At the end of each month he records his takings in a graph.

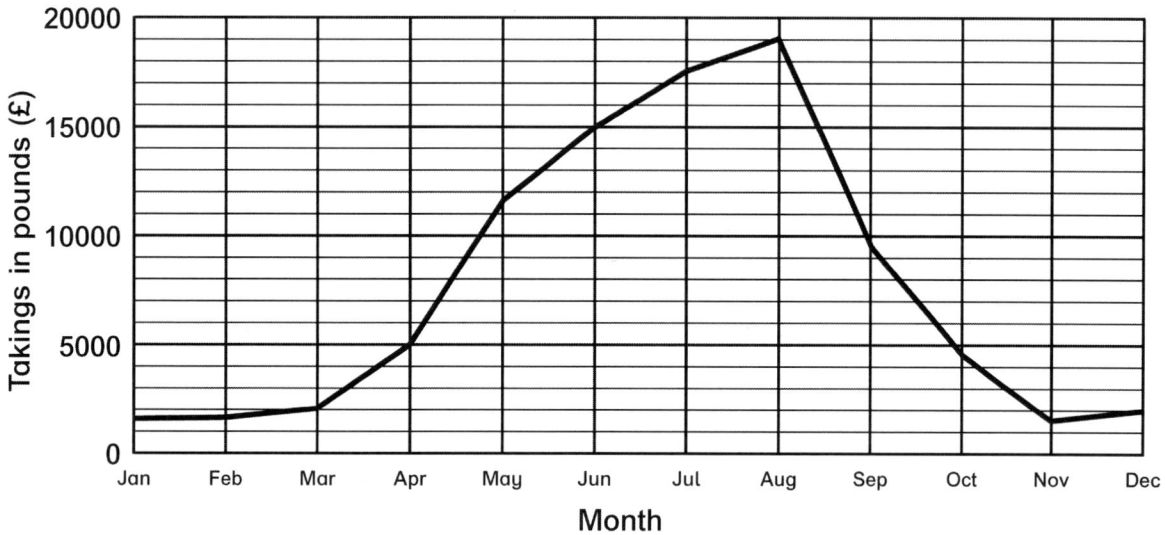

Answer these questions.

a) Estimate how much Mr White took in April.

£ _____

1 mark

b) Estimate how much Mr White took in June, July and August altogether.

£ _____

1 mark

c) Estimate how much more Mr White took in August than in January.

£ _____

1 mark

d) Estimate the fall in Mr White's takings from August to September.

£ _____

1 mark

Total for this page

2. This timetable shows the morning flights from Manchester to London.
The timetable shows the times and days of the flights.

Dep	Arr	Airline	Flight number	Mon	Tue	Wed	Thur	Fri	Sat	Sun
06:00	07:00	B.A.	BA1371	✓	✓			✓		
07:20	08:30	B.A.	BA1385						✓	
07:25	08:25	V.A.A.	VS3046	✓	✓	✓	✓	✓	✓	✓
07:25	08:35	B.A.	BA1385	✓	✓	✓	✓			✓
07:35	08:45	B.A.	BA1385					✓		
08:35	09:45	B.A.	BA1373			✓	✓			
08:50	10:00	B.A.	BA1387	✓	✓	✓	✓	✓		✓
09:50	11:00	B.A.	BA1389		✓				✓	✓
09:55	11:05	B.A.	BA1389	✓				✓		
10:40	11:40	V.A.A.	VS3042	✓	✓	✓	✓	✓	✓	✓
11:20	12:30	B.A.	BA1391	✓		✓				
11:25	12:35	B.A.	BA1391		✓		✓	✓		

Answer these questions.

a) What is the longest flight time?

_____

1 mark

b) How many flights to London are there on a Friday?

_____

1 mark

c) Dev arrives at Manchester Airport at 08:00 on Saturday for the next flight to London.
At what time will he arrive in London?

_____

1 mark

3. Calculate the mean of these numbers:

35   32   61   56   56

_____

1 mark

Total for this page

4. The mean of 4 numbers is 9.

A fifth number is added and the new mean is 10.

What was the fifth number?

_____

1 mark

5. Two schools have the same dinner menu.

They both offer:

● Chicken pie

○ Vegetarian sausages

◐ Jacket potato

● Sandwich

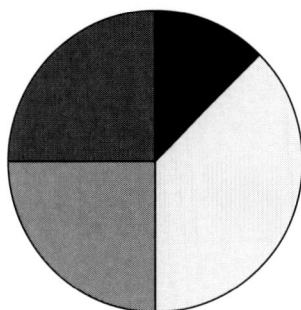

**Hillbury School
120 children**

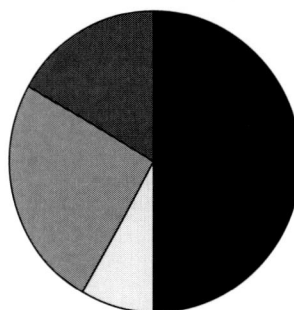

**Beckdale School
180 children**

Answer these questions.

a) Estimate the number of children at
Beckdale School who had chicken pie.

_____

1 mark

b) Estimate the number of children at Hillbury
School who had vegetarian sausage.

_____

1 mark

c) Tina looked at the pie charts and said, 'The same number of children
at both schools had jacket potato.'

Is Tina correct? Circle   YES   or   NO.

Explain your answer.

_____

_____

_____

1 mark

d) Tina also said, 'At Hillbury School the number of children who had a
sandwich or a jacket potato is the same as those who had a chicken
pie at Beckdale School.'

Is Tina correct? Circle   YES   or   NO.

Explain your answer.

_____

1 mark

_____

Total for
this page

_____

6. Four friends collect stickers.

The mean of the number of stickers is 156.

How many stickers do they have in total?

1 mark

7. Here are five number cards.

One card is face down.

12   14   23   12   ( )

The mean of the five numbers is 13.

What is the number on the card face down?

_____

1 mark

/15

Total for this test

118

Year 5
Statistics   Test 5: Mental mathematics

Instructions – to be read to pupils

Listen carefully to these instructions. I am going to ask you 20 questions. I will read each question twice. Listen carefully both times. You will then have time to work out your answer.

On your sheet there is an answer box for each question. Some questions are easy and some are harder. For some questions, important information is already written down for you on the sheet.

Work out the answer to each question in your head. Don't try to write down your calculations as this wastes time and you may miss the next question. If it helps you, you may jot things down outside the answer box.

If you can't work out an answer, put a cross in the answer box. If you make a mistake, cross out the wrong answer and then write the correct answer next to it.

You won't be able to ask questions once the test has begun. If you have any questions you may ask them now.

Now we are ready to start the test.

		Mark	Answer

For these questions, you will have 5 seconds to work out each answer and write it down.

		Mark	Answer
1.	Look at your answer sheet. Questions 1, 2 and 3 are all about this graph. Children in a class were asked about their first pet. The results were put in a bar chart. How many children owned rabbits?	1	7
2.	How many children owned a dog or a cat?	1	22
3.	How many more cats were owned than dogs?	1	2
4.	Look at your answer sheet. Questions 4 and 5 are about this graph. The pie chart shows the number of points won by different teams on a sports day. Which team won?	1	Green
5.	Which two teams had the same number of points?	1	Blue and yellow

For these questions, you will have 10 seconds to work out each answer and write it down.

		Mark	Answer
6.	Look at your answer sheet. This table shows numbers of boys and girls who played on a computer one night and those who did not. How many children did not play on a computer?	1	10
7.	Look at your answer sheet. This symbol represents 5 letters. What number of letters would be represented by 6 symbols like this?	1	30
8.	Look at your answer sheet. Questions 8, 9 and 10 are about this graph. This graph shows the depth of a river over some days of a thunderstorm. On which day do you think it rained?	1	Accept • Tuesday • Wednesday • Tuesday or Wednesday
9.	What was the depth of the river before the thunderstorm?	1	125 +/– 5
10.	By how many centimetres did the depth of the river go down between Wednesday and Friday?	1	75 +/– 5
11.	Look at your answer sheet. Questions 11 and 12 are about this graph. This graph is used to convert British pounds into American dollars. How many dollars are equivalent to 20 pounds?	1	30
12.	Estimate how many pounds are equivalent to 15 dollars.	1	10
13.	Look at your answer sheet. Questions 13, 14 and 15 are about this timetable. This is a timetable for trains from Manchester to Liverpool. What time does the 09:25 train from Manchester arrive in Widnes?	1	10:15
14.	How long does it take for a train to go from Manchester to Warrington?	1	40
15.	How long does it take for a train to go from Warrington to Liverpool?	1	20

For these questions, you will have 15 seconds to work out each answer and write it down.

16.	Look at your answer sheet. Questions 16 and 17 are about this table. The table shows the ages of members of a gym club and whether members are male or female. How many of the members are female?	1	280
17.	How many of the members are under 18 years of age?	1	80
18.	Calculate the mean of 4, 15, 1 and 8.	1	7
19.	The total of six numbers is 42. What is the mean?	1	7
20.	The mean of three numbers is 5. Two of the numbers are 1 and 9. What is the third?	1	5

Now put down your pen or pencil. The test is finished.

Test 5: Mental mathematics

Name: _____ Class: _____ Date: _____

5-second questions

1.

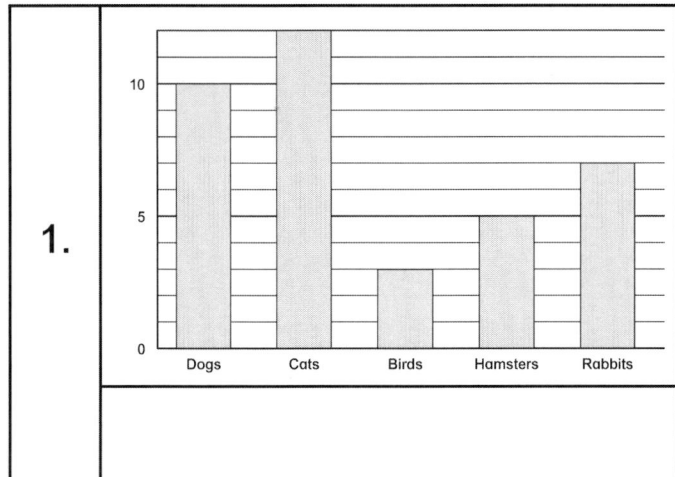

2.

3.

4.

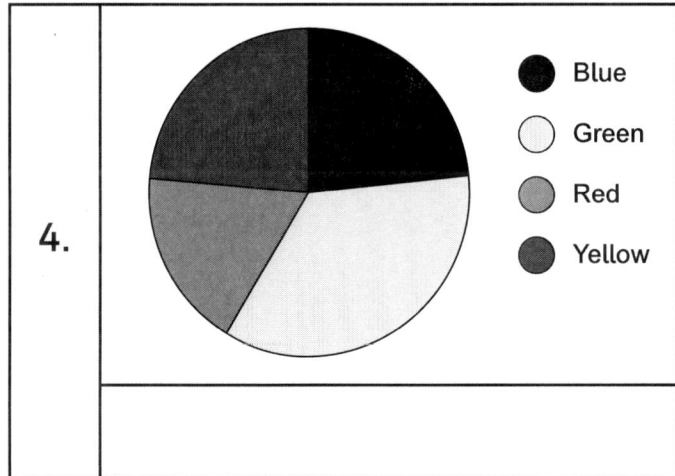

5.

10-second questions

6.

	Boys	Girls
Played on a computer	9	11
Did not play on a computer	8	2

7.

8.

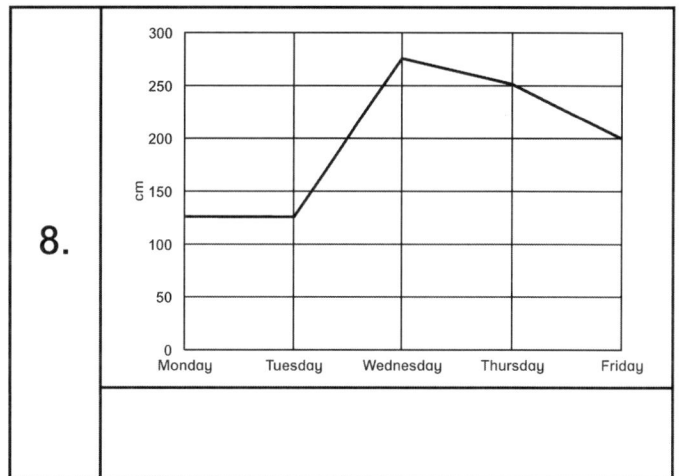

9. cm

10. cm

Year 5
Statistics

Test 5: Mental mathematics

Name: _____ Class: _____ Date: _____

11.

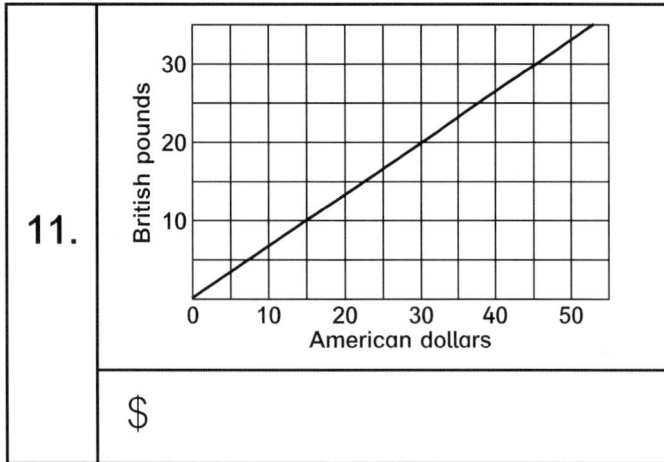

$

12. £

13.

Manchester	08:45	09:25	10:10
Warrington	09:25	10:05	10:50
Widnes	09:35	10:15	11:00
Liverpool	09:45	10:25	11:10

14. minutes

15. minutes

15-second questions

16.

	Male	Female
Under 18 years	45	35
18 – 30 years	120	105
31 years and over	110	140

17.

18.

19.

20.

Total for this test

/20

Answers and mark schemes

Year 5 Number and place value

Test 1(L)		Mark	Extra Information
1.	45, 72	1	Both numbers needed for mark
2.	24 742	1	
3.	0, –7	1	Both numbers needed for mark
4.	60 or 6 tens	1	
5.	5749, 6900, 7081, 10 006	1	
6.	4605	1	
7.	8100	1	
8.	27 605	1	
9.	496	1	
10.	2	1	
11.		1	Four correct lines needed for mark
12.	–4, –3, 0, 4, 5	1	
13.	5049	1	
14.	23	1	
15.	275	1	

Number and place value (continued)

Test 2(M)		Mark	Extra Information
1.	33 004, 32 895, 30 928, 29 860, 9879	1	
2.	Six hundred thousand, three hundred and nine	1	
3.	544 362	1	
4.	737 296	1	
5.	–14	1	
6.	Arrow pointing at 3	1	
7.	169 489 — 167 000 167 231 — 168 000 167 601 — 169 000 170 654 — 170 000 169 654 — 171 000	1	All correct lines needed for mark
8.	52 601	1	
9.	990 000	1	
10.	1000 or 1 thousand	1	
11.	843 710	1	
12.	–7	1	
13.	420 012	1	
14.	40 000 OR 40 thousand OR forty thousand	1	
15.	355 000	1	

Test 3(M)		Mark	Extra Information
1.	45 078	1	
2.	610 400	1	
3.	4005, 4007, 4050, 4070, 4500	1	
4.	34 795	1	
5.	30 075	1	
6.	900 000	1	
7.	–5	1	
8.	9	1	Do not accept –9°C
9.	–9, –18	1	Both answers needed for mark
10.	900 000	1	
11.	52 380, 52 400, 52 000	2	All three answers needed for 2 marks Any two answers needed for 1 mark
12.	2008	1	
13.	1000	1	
14.	68 301	1	

Number and place value (continued)

Test 4(H)	Mark	Extra Information
1. 5	1	Accept 50 000
2. 700 or 7 hundred or seven hundred	1	
3. 22	1	Do not accept −22°C
4. 466 000	1	
5. 1990	1	
6. 108 704	1	
7. 7, 4, −2, −5, −10	1	
8. 9 009 000	1	
9. 4 800 000	1	
10. 10	1	
11. 4 935 786, 4 937 830, 4 943 734, 4 947 243	1	
12. 64	1	
13. Third number circled or otherwise indicated only: 6 783 843	1	
14. 7	1	
15. 6 820 200	1	

Addition and subtraction

Test 1(L)	Mark	Extra Information
1. 5697	1	
2. 6360	1	
3. 9401	1	
4. 5044	1	
5. 8	1	
6. 26 059	1	
7. 10 250	2	Award 1 mark for a correct method but incorrect answer, e.g. 8499 – 3749 + 5500 = error
8. 23 092	1	
9. a) 80 000 b) 79 434	a) 1 b) 1	
10. 58 554	1	
11. 28 593 OR 115 275	1	
12. 76 325	1	
13. 59 243	1	

Test 2(M)	Mark	Extra Information
1. 59 942	1	
2. 59 062	1	
3. 94 074	1	
4. 40 905	1	
5. a) 30 000 b) 32 106	a) 1 b) 1	
6. 9877.79	1	
7. 607.18	1	
8. a) 55 305 b) 1171	a) 1 b) 1	
9. 1683	1	
10. 27 398 +32 735 60 133	1	
11. 50 000	1	
12. 55 678	2	Award 1 mark for a correct method but incorrect answer, e.g. 45 823 – 32 879 + 42 734 = error

Addition and subtraction (continued)

Test 3(M)	Mark	Extra Information
1. 341 225	1	
2. 615 298	1	
3. 317 072	1	
4. 660 128	1	
5. 76 200	1	
6. a) 573 000 b) 573 421	a) 1 b) 1	
7. 365 816	1	
8. 120 732	2	
9. 720 814	1	
10. 487 500	1	

11. 89 216
  −37 295
  51 921
	1	

12. a) 136 855 b) 49 351	a) 1 b) 1	

Test 4(H)	Mark	Extra Information
1. 586 761	1	
2. 397 184	1	
3. 1 215 782	1	
4. 216 869	1	
5. 78 383	1	
6. 220 000	1	
7. 16 154	1	
8. 20 760	2	Award 1 mark for a correct method but incorrect answer, e.g. 48 523 − (24 632 + 1655 + 1476) = error
9. £5000 and £14 400	2	Award 1 mark for a correct method but incorrect answer, e.g. (5000 + 6700 + 8400 + 11 450 + 13 450 + 14 400) − 40 000 = error
10. 49 439	1	
11. She should have rounded up, but she rounded them all down. Rounding up would give an estimated answer of 1 600 000.	1	
12. 67 803	2	Award 1 mark for a correct method but incorrect answer, e.g. (125 500 + 135 750 + 149 900 + 155 000) − (375 000 + 37 675 + 85 672) = error

Multiplication and division

Test 1(L)	Mark	Extra Information
1. a) $3 \times 4 = 12$ OR $4 \times 3 = 12$ b) $7 \times 8 = 56$ OR $8 \times 7 = 56$	a) 1 b) 1	
2. 2304	1	
3. 96	1	
4. 936	1	
5. 124	1	
6. 384	1	
7. 112	1	
8. 2, 4, 5, 10	1	
9. 1, 2, 3, 6	1	1 mark for any three correct OR the four correct answers plus one incorrect
10. 41, 43, 47 circled and no others	1	
11. 588	1	
12. 150	1	
13. 93.75	1	
14. 7	1	

Test 2(M)	Mark	Extra Information
1. 1, 2, 4, 8	1	1 mark for any three correct or the four correct answers plus one incorrect
2. 24, 48, OR any multiple of 24 ... 72, 96, 120 ...	1	Two answers needed for the mark
3. 25×6 or 30×5 or 50×3 or 75×2	1	
4. 37 512	1	
5. 1296	1	
6. 53, 59 circled and no others	1	
7. ~~456 000~~ *4560*	1	
8. 312	1	Do not accept 312 r 4, 312.5, $312\frac{4}{8}$ or $312\frac{1}{2}$
9. 256	2	Award 1 mark for a correct method but incorrect answer, e.g. 192 x 4 = error error ÷ 3
10. 36, 225 circled and no others	1	
11. 4 7 3 8 $\times$ 7 3 3 1 6 6	1	
12. 3 + 17 or 17 + 3 7 + 13 or 13 + 7	1	Two different pairs of numbers needed for 1 mark.
13. Explanation needs to show that doubling 3 450 000 and adding half of 3 450 000 would provide the answer.	1	
14. 30	1	

Multiplication and division (continued)

Test 3(M)		Mark	Extra Information
1.		2	Award 1 mark for five or six numbers correctly placed
2. 280, 560, 1120		1	Both numbers circled for 1 mark
3. 332 522		1	
4. 632.75		1	Accept 632.75, $632\frac{6}{8}$, $632\frac{3}{4}$, 632 r 6
5. 2, 3, 5		1	Accept numbers in any order Accept numbers as a list
6. a) 5500 b) 670		1	Both answers for 1 mark
7. 2500 ml of mineral water 250 g of sugar 200 ml of lemon juice		1	Accept other units of measure, e.g. 2.5 l only if ml is deleted and replaced with l
8. 355		1	
9. **81** is a square number. **27** is a cube number. **64** is both a square and a cube number.		1	All correct for 1 mark
10. 8 100 AND sight of evidence of use of given fact, e.g. 5400 × 1.5 OR 5400 + 2700		1	Award 1 mark for evidence of correct method (as shown on left)
11. 74		1	
12. 377		1	Do not accept 377.7, 377.77, $377\frac{7}{9}$ or 377 r 7
13. 55 636		1	
14. 725		1	

Table for question 1:

	Multiple of 3	Not a multiple of 3
Factor of 24	3, 6	2, 4, 8
Not a factor of 24	9	5, 7

Test 4(H)		Mark	Extra Information
1. 24		1	Accept 144, 264, 384 … (sequence adds 120)
2. 536 696		1	
3. 1396.5		1	Accept 1396.5, $1396\frac{3}{6}$, $1396\frac{1}{2}$ or 1396 r 3
4. 2981		1	
5. 11, 13, 17, 19		1	All numbers needed for 1 mark
6. 1, 2, 3, 6, 7, 14, 21, 42		2	Accept for 1 mark any six or seven correct answers
7. 306 480		1	
8. 146.5		1	Accept 146.5, $146\frac{16}{32}$, $146\frac{1}{2}$ or 146 r 16
9. 560 and 728 circled and no others		1	
10. 322 840		1	
11. a) Shop 1 by £108 b) 103 812	a) 1 b) 1		
12. a) 420 000 b) 427 392	a) 1 b) 1		

Fractions, decimals and percentages

Test 1(L)	Mark	Extra Information
1. 24	1	
2. $\frac{2}{10}$ or $\frac{1}{5}$	1	
3. 4 tenths	1	
4. 5.4, 5.5, 5.7, 6.3, 6.5, 6.6 matched to 5, 6, 7	1	All correct lines needed for 1 mark
5. 13.12, 12.64, 12.48, 12.43, 11.96	1	
6. $1\frac{1}{2}$ or $\frac{3}{2}$	1	
7. 0.2, 0.75, 0.25, 0.5 matched to $\frac{1}{2}$, $\frac{1}{4}$, $\frac{3}{4}$, $\frac{1}{5}$	1	All correct lines needed for 1 mark
8. $\frac{7}{12}, \frac{2}{3}, \frac{19}{24}, \frac{5}{6}$	1	Accept $\frac{14}{24}, \frac{16}{24}, \frac{19}{24}, \frac{20}{24}$
9. 3	1	
10. $\frac{2}{4}$, $\frac{5}{4}$, $\frac{3}{4}$, $\frac{1}{4}$ matched to $1\frac{1}{4}$, $\frac{1}{2}$, $\frac{5}{8}$, $\frac{3}{12}$, $\frac{6}{8}$	2	Award 1 mark for one or two correct lines
11. $1\frac{1}{8}$	1	Accept $\frac{9}{8}$
12. $\frac{23}{100}$	1	
13. 364.21	1	
14. 70	1	

Fractions, decimals and percentages (continued)

Test 2(M)	Mark	Extra Information
1. $\frac{7}{8}, \frac{3}{4}, \frac{11}{16}, \frac{1}{2}$	1	Accept $\frac{14}{16}, \frac{12}{16}, \frac{11}{16}, \frac{8}{16}$
2. $\frac{70}{100} = \frac{7}{10}$	1	Both missing numerators need to be correct for 1 mark
3. <table><tr><th>Improper fraction</th><th>Mixed number</th></tr><tr><td>$\frac{5}{4}$</td><td>$1\frac{1}{4}$</td></tr><tr><td>$\frac{23}{6}$</td><td>$3\frac{5}{6}$</td></tr><tr><td>$\frac{42}{5}$</td><td>$8\frac{2}{5}$</td></tr></table>	2	
4. $\frac{4}{12}$ or $\frac{1}{3}$	1	
5. $1\frac{3}{5}$	1	
6. $\frac{1}{2}$ $\frac{5}{10}$ $\frac{50}{100}$	1	All three fractions circled for the mark and no others
7. 4.85, 5.05	1	Both answers for 1 mark
8. 7.8 3.2	1	Both answers for 1 mark
9. Explanation needs to show that 13.3 is larger because it has $\frac{3}{10}$ while 13.13 only has $\frac{1}{10}$ and $\frac{3}{100}$ or 13.3 is larger because it has $\frac{30}{100}$ while 13.13 only has $\frac{13}{100}$.	1	No mark for just indicating 13.3 is the larger number
10. 72.37	1	
11. 5	1	
12. 50	1	
13. 14.6	1	
14. 0.102, 0.122, 0.201, 0.211, 0.212	1	

Test 3(M)	Mark	Extra Information
1. $\frac{13}{20}$	1	
2. 2	1	
3. $2\frac{3}{8}$	1	
4. $1\frac{3}{8}$	1	
5. $7\frac{1}{2}$	1	Accept $\frac{15}{2}$
6. $\frac{5}{100}$	1	
7. $\frac{9}{1000} + \frac{3}{100} + \frac{6}{10}$	1	
8. 15.49, 14.7	1	Both numbers circled and no others
9. 0.71, 0.731, 3.137, 3.37, 3.7	1	
10. 77.6	1	
11. 35	1	
12. <table><tr><th>Fraction</th><th>Decimal</th><th>Percentage</th></tr><tr><td>$\frac{1}{2}$</td><td>0.5</td><td>50%</td></tr><tr><td>$\frac{1}{4}$</td><td>0.25</td><td>25%</td></tr><tr><td>$\frac{2}{5}$</td><td>0.4</td><td>40%</td></tr></table>	2	Award 1 mark for three numbers correctly placed
13. 0.75, 75	1	
14. $\frac{9}{12}$ or $\frac{3}{4}$	1	

Fractions, decimals and percentages (continued)

Test 4(H)	Mark	Extra Information
1. $\frac{1}{6}, \frac{1}{3}, \frac{9}{24}, \frac{5}{12}$	1	Accept $\frac{4}{24}, \frac{8}{24}, \frac{9}{24}, \frac{10}{24}$
2. 5	1	
3. $\frac{8}{10}$	1	Accept $\frac{4}{5}$
4. 14.28 and 14.34	1	Both numbers and no others circled for mark
5. 5.25	1	
6. 29.7	1	
7. 600	1	
8. $\frac{10}{15}, \frac{16}{24}, \frac{12}{18}$	1	All three numbers circled and no others.
9. $7\frac{9}{10}$	1	
10. $\frac{8}{15}$	1	
11. $\frac{1}{12}$	1	
12. 0.125	1	
13.	1	All four answers correct for mark
14.	1	All four answers correct for mark
15. $1\frac{3}{4}, 2\frac{1}{4}, 2\frac{1}{2}, 2\frac{5}{8}, 2\frac{3}{4}$	1	Accept equivalent fractions

13.

	÷10	÷100
45.2	4.52	0.452
307.4	30.74	3.074
72	7.2	0.72

14.

	×10	×100
5.6	56	560
0.603	6.03	60.3
2.007	20.07	200.7

Measurement

Test 1(L)	Mark	Extra Information
1. 35	1	
2. 40	1	
3. 14	1	
4. 1980	1	Accept 1.98 l
5. 6:15 p.m. 8:35 p.m.	1	Both times (including p.m.) needed for 1 mark
6. 21	1	
7. $3\frac{1}{4} l$	1	
8. Yes Explanation needs to show an understanding of place value – the 6 has moved one column to the left, which makes it ten times larger	1	Explanations not sufficient for the mark: • Yes • Because it's ten times bigger
9. 1.65(0)	2	Award 1 mark for a correct method but incorrect answer, e.g. (5.5 × 30) ÷ 100 = error
10. 60	1	
11. 8	1	
12. 8	1	
13. 206	1	
14. Arrow OR line indicating 75 ml	1	Accept any line >70ml and <75ml

Test 2(M)	Mark	Extra Information
1. 7 kg, 1.7 kg, $\frac{3}{4}$ kg, 700 g, 0.25 kg	1	
2. 0.3 m, 30 cm	1	
3. 4.48 l	1	
4. 40	1	
5. 84	2	Award 1 mark for a correct method but incorrect answer, e.g. 36 ÷ 6 = error error × 14
6. 9.5	1	
7. 36 cm^2	1	Correct units required for 1 mark
8. 2	1	
9. 30	1	
10. 492	1	
11. 205	1	
12. 10	1	
13. 20.80	2	Award 1 mark for a correct method but incorrect answer, e.g. (1.85 × 4) + (2.35 × 2) + (2.90 × 3) = error

Measurement (continued)

Test 3(M)	Mark	Extra Information
1. 60 600	1	Both answers needed for 1 mark
2. Line drawn at 400 ml	1	
3. 5.5 or $5\frac{1}{2}$	1	
4. 90	1	
5. 36	1	1 mark for showing 5 (of the 6) correct side lengths, i.e. clockwise from the top: 10, 5, 6, 3, 4, 8 Accept the shortcut that says it's the same as the larger rectangle for 1 mark
6. 11	1	
7. **A** = 9.5 cm²; **B** = 8.5 cm² Difference is 1 cm²	2	Award 1 mark for: • Two correct areas for A and B • One correct area and correct difference using incorrect area
8. Accept any amount >270, <300	1	
9. 24	1	
10. 300	1	
11. 3	1	
12. 2.8 m or 280 cm or 2 m 80 cm	1	
13. 6.50	2	Award 1 mark for reaching a total of £43.50 OR Award 1 mark for a correct method, e.g. 50 − [(4.35 × 2) + (6.50 × 4) + (4.40 × 2)]

Test 4(H)	Mark	Extra Information
1. 20 mm, 2.5 cm, 2.05 m, 250 cm	1	
2. 10	1	
3. 3.35	1	
4. 16	1	Accept 0.16 m if cm changed
5. 112	2	Award 1 mark for a correct method, e.g. 2(11 + 15 + 12 + 18) or 2(11 + 15) + 2(12 + 18)
6. 3600 seconds	1	
7. 42 cm, 450 mm, 5200 mm, 5.5 m, 0.006 km	1	
8. 50	1	
9. 320	1	
10. 26 or 16	1	
11. Accept any of the following: 9, 16, 21, 24, 25	1	
12. 42	1	
13. 120	1	
14. 500	1	

Geometry

Test 1(L)	Mark	Extra Information
1. Ticks 2nd triangle	1	
2. Ticks angle on top row on right	1	
3. 4	1	
4.	1	
5. (6, 5)	1	
6. 4 right, 3 down	1	Instructions can be listed in either order
7. (4, 2)	1	
8. Triangular prism	1	
9.	1	
10. 125	1	Allow answers in the range 123° to 127°
11. Ticks equilateral triangle, square and hexagon only	1	
12. 30	1	Accept answers in the range 25° to 35° inclusive
13. Accept answers of 70° +/− 2°	1	
14. 120	1	
15. 20	1	

Geometry (continued)

Test 2(M)		Mark	Extra Information
1.		1	
2.	Cuboid	1	
3.	160	1	Accept answers in the range 150° to 170°
4.	Accept answers of 135 +/− 2	1	
5.	112	1	
6.	202	1	
7.	18	2	Award 1 mark for a correct method but incorrect answer, e.g. $\dfrac{90 - (27 \times 2)}{2}$ = error
8.	$s = 55$ $t = 35$	2	Award 1 mark for one correct angle
9.	Ticks triangle	1	
10.		1	
11.	Answer needs to explain that the sides AND/OR angles are different.	1	
12.	72	1	
13.	16	1	

Geometry (continued)

Test 3(M)		Mark	Extra Information
1.	Square-based pyramid	1	Accept pyramid
2.	Triangular prism	1	
3.		1	
4.	Acute, right, obtuse, reflex	1	All four correct answers for 1 mark
5.	a) $b = 105 +/- 5$ b) $c = 255 +/- 5$	a) 1 b) 1	For c, accept $360 - b$
6.	Correctly drawn angle of 145° +/− 2°	1	
7.	270	1	
8.		2	Award 1 mark for one shape correctly drawn. OR Award 1 mark for two shapes in the correct orientation but incorrectly placed on the grid
9.	22.5 or $22\frac{1}{2}$	1	
10.	45	1	
11.	Ticks rhombus	1	
12.	5	1	
13.	15	1	

Geometry (continued)

Test 4(H)	Mark	Extra Information
1. mirror line	1	
2. Cylinder	1	
3. B, D, A, E, C	1	
4. Angle drawn of 165° +/− 2°	1	Leave space for an angle to be drawn on answer sheet
5. 93	1	
6. 67	1	
7. The hexagon has 6 angles; each one is 120°	1	
8. Accurately drawn triangle: • Base: 12 cm • +/− 2 mm • Angles: 65°, 37° and 78° • +/− 2°	1	
9. Any one net from the options below:	1	
10. a) 23 b) 22	a) 1 b) 1	
11. 48	1	
12. A = radius B = circumference C = diameter	2	2 marks for three correct answers 1 marks for two correct answers
13. r = 108 s = 72 t = 108	1	

Statistics

Test 1(L)	Mark	Extra Information
1. a) 30 +/– 3 b) 300 +/– 3	a) 1 b) 1	
2. a) Saturday to Sunday b) 55 c) 8 +/– 1	a) 1 b) 1 c) 1	c) Accept answers in the range 7–9 inclusive
3. a) 11 b) 4	a) 1 b) 1	
4. a) 11:00 (a.m.) to 12:00 (p.m.) b) 6 +/– 1 c) Accept any reasonable explanation, such as: • The heating was turned down. • The doors/windows were open. • The children left the classroom for lunch.	a) 1 b) 1 c) 1	a) Accept 11:00 (a.m.) or 12:00 (p.m.) individually.
5. a) 43 b) 34 c) 48	a) 1 b) 1 c) 1	
6. a) 64 b) 95	a) 1 b) 1	

Test 2(M)	Mark	Extra Information
1. a) An amount >1510, <1590 b) March and September c) Explanation needs to say that the amount of money in the school fund stayed the same OR the amount of money spent equalled the amount of money put into the fund d) Explanation needs to show that the amount of money donated was less than the amount of money spent.	a) 1 b) 1 c) 1 d) 1	
2. a) 9.00 b) 21.00 c) 86.25	a) 2 b) 1 c) 1	Award 1 mark for a correct method but incorrect answer, e.g. [(12.75 × 2) + (5.75 × 2)] − 28 = error
3. a) 2 000 000 or 2 million +/– 200 000 b) 1971 and 1981 c) 63 000 000 or 63 million +/– 500 000	a) 1 b) 1 c) 1	c) Accept >62.5 million, <64 million
4. a) 3 hours 12 minutes b) 18:42 c) 15:25 d) 3 hours 12 minutes or 192 minutes	a) 1 b) 1 c) 1 d) 1	

Statistics (continued)

Test 3(M)	Mark	Extra Information

1. a) i) Chris
    ii) 14(%) +/− 2(%)
b) i) Mick
    ii) 30(%) +/− 2(%)
c) ⩾42%, <45%
d) 11th Oct(ober) and 8th Nov(ember)
	a) 1
	
	b) 1
	
	c) 1
	d) 1
		For **a)** and **b)** no marks awarded for just naming Chris and Mick

2. a) 2 hours 45 minutes or 165 minutes +/− 5 minutes b) Casualty c) 12:45 am +/− 5 minutes d) 4:40 p.m. +/− 5 minutes	a) 1 b) 1 c) 1 d) 1	**c)** Accept 00:45, 12:45, 12:45 a.m., quarter ($\frac{1}{4}$) to one (1) Do not accept 12:45 p.m. **d)** Accept 16:40, 4:40, 4:40 p.m., twenty (20) to five (5) Do not accept 4:40 a.m.
3. a) >10.25, ⩽11 b) >12.75, ⩽13 c) ⩾11, ⩽12 d) ⩾4, ⩽6	a) 1 b) 1 c) 1 d) 1	**b)** Accept answers in the range >9.75, <10.25
4. a) 1 hour 23 minutes or 83 minutes b) 09:43 c) 48	a) 1 b) 1 c) 1	

Test 4(H)	Mark	Extra Information
1. a) 5000 b) >50 000, <53 000 c) >17 000, <18 000 d) <10 000 and >9 000	a) 1 b) 1 c) 1 d) 1	
2. a) 1 hour 10 minutes or 70 minutes b) 7 c) 11:00 a.m.	a) 1 b) 1 c) 1	**a)** Both answers needed for 1 mark
3. 48	1	
4. 14	1	
5. a) 90 b) 45 +/− 5 c) Explanation should show that the number of children having jacket potato at Beckdale School is 45 ($\frac{1}{4}$ of 180) and at Hillbury School is 30 ($\frac{1}{4}$ of 120), so Tina is incorrect. d) Explanation should show that at Hillbury School, $\frac{1}{4}$ had a sandwich and $\frac{1}{4}$ had a jacket potato, which is $\frac{1}{2}$ and half of 180 children is 90. At Beckdale School, $\frac{1}{2}$ had a chicken pie and half of 120 children is 60. So Tina is incorrect.	a) 1 b) 1 c) 1 d) 1	**b)** Accept numbers in the range 42–48 inclusive
6. 624	1	
7. 4	1	